North

New Moon

Balsamic

Waxing Crescent

Capricorn
♑
MIDNIGHT

Aquarius
♒

Sagittarius
♐

Winter Solstice

Scorpio
♏

Samhain

Imbolc

Pisces
♓

First Quarter

West

Libra
♎
6:00 PM

Autumnal Equinox

Aries
♈
6:00 AM

Spring Equinox

East

Last Quarter

Virgo
♍

Lughnasad

Beltane

Taurus
♉

Disseminating

Leo
♌

Summer Solstice

NOON

Cancer
♋

Gemini
♊

Gibbous

Full Moon

South

Natural Rhythms™

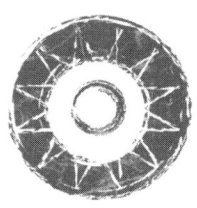

"Lisa's visionary guidance about the Natural Rhythms and the Elemental Forces led me back to my innate wisdom and spiritual center. This work is filled wih vital, powerful tools I did not learn in medical school and I am thrilled to have these new insights to share with my patients. These are cutting edge concepts for deeper emotional, spiritual and physical health."
Tammy Huber-Wilkins MD, Psychiatrist

"Lisa Michael's goal is to educate and guide humanity to dance to the tune of its true inner potential. Get ready! With this book you'll find yourself making extraordinary moves and doing wondrous things."
William Henry, investigative mythologist, author, co-host of "Dreamland" radio program.

"In Natural Rhythms, Lisa Michaels lovingly unfolds an exquisite treatise on the sacred systems of nature and the cosmic order. This magnificent work demystifies and unifies these great mysteries in utterly accessible stories and explanations. Then, as it shines a clarifying light on the beauty of the natural world's rhythmic design, it offers us practical insight into our own lives, providing an array of exercises to increase our alignment with these powerful energies."
Bonnie Sparling - Writer, Teacher

"Natural Rhythms comes forth in perfect timing when Integrative/Holistic Medicine is seeking balance between all their technological knowledge and desperately attempting to piece into their modalities the innate natural cycles of nature to assist in Healing Humankind and the Planet."
Susan F. Kersey, RN, M.Ed ~ Wholistic Educational Wellness Consultant

"My experience with Natural Rhythms and Lisa Michaels, has helped me to de-velop a unique blend of inner/outer world capacities by more deeply connecting with nature. Lisa's organized system is filled easy and practical applications for anyone wanting to hear the whispers of the soul and discover their own inner dancer."
Leslie Clayton ~ Dancer and Owner Body Awareness Studio

"I've known Lisa Michaels for a number of years, and her work is amazing. Her teachings are easy to understand, and powerful to practice. She is a wonderful teacher, and yet she continues to be a student herself. She's somebody who constantly hones her craft."
Jerry Miner ~ Source Books

"When we are operating in resonance with the natural cycles and rhythms of our world, magic happens! When we open our hearts and our awareness to these mysteries we become co-creative participants in the magic of life."
Cayelin K Castell ~ Co-Author Shamanic Astrology Handbook

"Lisa Michaels explains patterns and rhythms in ways that speak to me on many levels, from cellular to cosmic. Get ready to "dance in your life" in deeper and richer ways!"
Claudia E. Harsh, M.D.,
Director of Integrative Gynecology, Alliance Institute for Integrative Medicine,

"Lisa synthesizes a number of potent transformational tools in her work with ease, grace and enthusiasm....her masterful teachings empower participants to fly on their own!"
Anyaa McAndrew, MA, NCC, LPC

"Natural Rhythms dynamically brings the energetic quality of each of the elements to life."
Nicole Christine ~ Author Under Her Wings

Natural Rhythms™

Connect the Creational Dance of Your Life to the Pulse of the Universe

LISA MICHAELS

Institute of Conscious Expression Company

Atlanta, Georgia

Natural Rhythms™
Connect the Creational Dance of Your Life to the Pulse of the Universe.

Copyright 2008 By Lisa Michaels.
All Rights Reserved.

This book, or parts thereof, may not be used or reproduced in any manner whatsoever without written permission except in the case of brief quotations in articles and reviews. Photocopies of the worksheets are allowed for personal use only.

For information, address Institute of Conscious Expression Co.
PO Box 3654, Lilburn, GA 30048.

Although every precaution has been taken in preparation of this book,
the publisher and author assume no responsibility for errors and omissions.

FIRST EDITION

Cover, Book Design and Illustrations: Prescott Hill
Main Editor: Nina Amir
Supporting Editors: Nicole Christine and Bonnie Sparling

Natural Rhythms™ is the trademark of Lisa Michaels.

Library of Congress Catalog Control Number: 2008922344

ISBN: 0-9715994-3-2

Printed in the United States of America

Other works by Lisa Michaels

The Elemental Forces of Creation Oracle

The Elemental Forces of Creation

Priestess Within

*The above titles are available at select bookstores
or may be ordered by visiting the
Institute of Conscious Expression Company
www.consciousexpression.com*

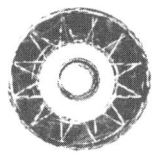

Four precious and vital mentors assisted my development by

taking me under their wings at just the right time.

With deep gratitude, I dedicate this book to these beautiful beings.

Thank you Diane, Jean Ann, Gail, and Nicole. Your teaching,

guidance, support, and loving care made my rich life expression

and this work possible.

Table of Contents

Natural Rhythms

"Dancing is the loftiest, the most moving,

the most beautiful of the arts, because it is not mere

translation or abstraction from life;

it is life itself."

Havelock Ellis

*I*n my life I have passionately loved two things, dance and spirituality. I grew up on the outskirts of Atlanta, Georgia before the growth boom of the '80s. I tenderly remember digging potatoes from the garden of my grandparents, playing outside for hours, attending the local Baptist church, and choreographing dances for my siblings and the neighborhood children. From a young age, I loved dancing and showed a natural aptitude for this artistic expression.

I recall riding my bike around the neighborhood asking God questions about my life. Before the mature age of twelve, I struggled deeply with one big question: "If I love dancing so much, how can it be considered a sin?" I had a hard time believing what I heard at church and in Sunday School about the activity I loved so much.

I didn't know then that this question, and all the questions that spun off from it over the years, would lead me on a lifelong journey. Nor did I realize that the journey would be one of inner and outer connection of significant magnitude. What I did know then was how much dancing meant to me, and when I posed that question to my mother, she said, "Lisa, if God gave you a talent, he meant for you to use it." Her answer profoundly supported my process of discovery, and those simple words kept me dancing as I struggled to reconcile my spiritual and physical worlds. A few years later, my father influenced my journey as well. He suggested I read my first personal growth book, which fueled my inner quest for expansion.

In the years that followed, I traveled two seemingly different paths. I went to college to dance and to train to become a dance teacher and, in any spare time I had, I actively pursued my love of spirituality and personal development. During college, I discovered how my personal development thrives with support and guidance as I connected to the first of a life-long series of powerful mentors, my dance teacher and company director, Diane Callahan.

After graduating from college, I continued on these two paths of dance and personal spiritual development. I moved to California and began sorting through the most effective ways of teaching ballet to young children. I created what would later become my syllabus for early childhood classes. In addition, for several years I directed a local performing company. I also found an amazing spiritual development teacher, Jean Ann Burger. Studying with a group of people for over five years, I developed some of my dearest and most lasting friendships. As a group, we went to see other powerful teachers of consciousness too. I flourished in this atmosphere of love, acceptance, and spiritual nourishment, and this helped me in my career as well.

As you may know, spiritual development happens in cycles. You do the inner work and then need to take that inner work into the outer world to practice using it. Once the inner and outer work have integrated, you can begin on the next level of growth. After five years of inner work with my teacher and my group of friends, I could feel that it was time for my next step. Just a few weeks after saying this to my teacher, my grandmother died, and I traveled back to Georgia for her funeral. After my visit, I felt the pull towards growth and realized I needed to return to the land of trees, rain, and family; all things I had missed while living in California. The pull toward growth, however, was also taking me away from something I genuinely loved, my spiritual family.

During that time, my consciousness began an interesting shift that only continued to deepen. I started longing for the spiritual voice of the feminine. Until that point, the only spiritual voice that I had heard had been masculine. I had been raised on "Father God" and a divine being referred to as "He," but now I needed to hear the feminine voice of God. In response to this longing, my spiritual path during those years turned toward the natural world and the Goddess. Later, both Goddess and God found room in my consciousness. As with many other things, as the years passed I discovered an inner place large enough for both the voice of the Divine Feminine and the Divine Masculine.

After my move back to Georgia, I spent a few years teaching dance and choreographing on a freelance basis. Eventually, I became the co-owner and director of a five hundred pupil ballet school, and I wrote and/or produced four dance syllabi and three compact discs of music for classroom movement. My products were featured in and on the cover of *Dance Teacher Now* magazine three times and were used in hundreds of schools across the country. During that time, I was applying the spiritual principles I had learned outside of the dance world to the dance classroom and to the business of running a dance school, and they obviously were working well.

More than that, however, my connection to the Divine Feminine, the Goddess, was leading me toward a new type of dance. I started inviting friends to dances at the school, and we did what I would call "expressive dance." We simply listened to music and moved in whatever way our bodies wanted. We had a wonderful time dancing in full circle skirts and flowing silk scarves, which helped us express ourselves even more.

I started taking that type of movement into my ballet classes to see how the children would respond. I realized very quickly that when I asked the children to dance in this way, I needed to provide a safe emotional environment for them to be able to open up to express themselves physically. They were used to the security of knowing the steps, so being asked to move expressively brought up their self-consciousness, their fears of being judged by their peers. I then began exploring ways of creating a safe environment for personal expression, an environment that allows people to move in new ways, expressing their deepest feelings and the essence of who they are.

Around the same time, I also started conducting ceremonies for myself and my friends to honor the changes of the seasons, and I began to get much more in harmony with nature. The ceremonies I created always included lots of free movement, to bring into the physical realm the energy of the intent on a spiritual, emotional, and intellectual level. In the dance classroom, I began to see more of the tremendous gifts that ballet had brought to my life. In fact, my ballet training and experience had both developed my consciousness and my physical body.

I realized that structured dance develops consciousness from the outside in. Dancers see and hear the dance instruction and apply it to their bodies, creating the appropriate dance shape and form, and they move their bodies in time to the music. This increases the dancer's physical coordination, their patterned thinking ability, and their capacity for harmonic synergy. Learning to beautifully coordinate physical movement in time to the music expands the brain's ability to effectively function on multiple levels at one time. I call this level of consciousness *harmonic synergy.*

Pictured left to right:

Nicole Christine, Lisa Michaels and Jean Ann Burger

Expressive dance works in the opposite direction -- from the inside out. It connects to the wellspring of creativity in the inner landscape of the dancer and then brings that ability to the outer world, thus increasing the capacity for creative problem solving, innovation, and personal expression. It became clear to me that when we develop the capacity to effectively work with what seems like two completely different expressions, coordinated dance and expressive dance, we increase our wholeness. We increase our ability to use both sides of our brain more effectively by learning a coordinated dance skill and doing expressive movement, patterned thinking, and creativity.

I was making these kinds of discoveries as I began to feel another call for the expansion of my development. Once again, to take my next step I had to leave something I loved — this time the ballet school. I adored my students, the dancing, the music, the performances, the costumes, the business, and the teaching, but it was time to go. The cycle I had been in was ending, and it was time for another cycle to begin. So, I sold my portion of the school and eventually sold the product portion of the business, too.

In the years during the sale of the school and immediately following, I thrived intellectually and developmentally, while emotionally I entered a dark night of the soul. It took me years to fully comprehend the impact my emotions had on my life experiences. I began an emotional healing journey that has both assisted me in my personal life and given me the necessary tools to work with others as they seek their own emotional healing. My emotional journey helped me develop the gift of compassion, so that as others passed through their own dark nights, I was able to support them more fully. I would find this skill very necessary in the years ahead.

While my emotional life went into a deep healing phase, other aspects of my life continued expanding. During the summer after selling the school, I was introduced to something called Accelerated Learning, which would impact all my future facilitation and teaching endeavors. Accelerated Learning is a teaching and facilitation method that engages the student in the learning process in ways they can more easily, and immediately, integrate and access the subject matter.

A dear friend of mine introduced me to a long-time friend of hers, Gail Heidenhain, who had been training others in this method for years. Gail was living in Germany at the time, and the only place she was soon to teach the course was in the Czech Republic. I was so eager to attend that I flew to Germany, and drove with her and her co-facilitator to the first of my many courses in Accelerated Learning. The style of facilitation taught by Accelerated Learning opened many doors for me and has been key to my comprehension of the concepts presented in this book.

During the transition years following the sale of the school, I also started taking courses and trainings on a wide variety of topics. I enjoyed them all, and each of them assisted my growth in one area or another. I took the Trance Dance Facilitator Training, studied emotional development at the Hendrick's Institute, began learning Shamanic Astrology, and went to various courses, workshops, and conferences with cutting edge leaders of consciousness. I also traveled on spiritual journeys to Peru, Egypt, Southern France, and the Yucatan.

My interest in the Divine Feminine remained strong during this time, and I focused on my desire to find a teacher of feminine consciousness. My desire was answered when a friend called me about a women's circle process coming to Atlanta: The Priestess Process, developed by Nicole Christine. I discovered this process assists people in deeply connecting to their inner guidance and wisdom, and to become their own direct channel for spirit.[1] Nicole profoundly influenced my life, and the Priestess Process opened me up spiritually in a way nothing previously had accomplished. Thus, I was able to begin bringing through my subconscious and into my consciousness my own body of knowledge, my work, and eventually I started facilitating The Priestess Process myself.

To do this, I had to initially remove the old cultural overlays from the word "priestess." I had to understand that a priestess or priest is simply a person with a direct connection to the Divine, and all of us have the capacity to develop that connection within. As I did this, that connection opened inside me, and I felt the expansion of my consciousness and of my abilities.

While taking the second level of the Priestess Process training, I stayed with Jean Ann my spiritual teacher/mentor in California. Before going to sleep one night we were talking, and I explained to her that I had been studying a wide range of seemingly unrelated topics for over twenty years. I knew by then how my own process worked, and I shared that with her: I tend to gather a wide variety of information and experiences and only later see how they all connect and work together. I decided to ask that night to be shown while sleeping how all the subjects I had intensely studied were related.

I woke up the next morning, picked up a napkin and pen, and drew four circles -- one circle for earth, one for water, one for air, and one for fire. In an instant, I understood how everything I had learned fit together: all the topics and areas of study fit into one of the elemental forces and their teachings. In that moment, I also knew how they each functioned in my consciousness. I would grow to understand so much more about this over the years.

The circles represented a flower and its petals. Just as each flower petal opens in its own time, separate from the other petals, it remains part of the whole flower. And the flower's beauty is dependent upon each and every petal. The same can be said of the development of a person's consciousness.

Most of us understand one or two concepts (petals) at a time, even though we previously have learned many more than this. Then a moment comes when the entire pattern of what we have learned unfolds completely before us (all the petals open), as if the puzzle pieces have all been put together, the patches all stitched into a quilt, or the chapters placed into a coherent book. This represents the flower at its most beautiful stage -- when all the petals are open.

So it was for me. I studied and developed spiritually for years - with one petal or two opening at a time, allowing for me to understand how they worked together. It wasn't until that morning that all the petals opened at the same time, that I could see the beauty and begin to understand the overall flower I had been studying. In my case, the flower I was studying actually was what is called The Flower of Life,[2] the symbol for the pattern of creation. The circles I had drawn were, in fact, the first four circles of The Flower of Life, which has Spirit as the rich substance flowing between the elements (Earth, Water, Air, and Fire) and holding them in form. What I now know is that the unfoldment of Spirit in matter happens in the same way a flower opens, consciousness unfolds, or a dancer learns to dance with harmonic synergy.

Initially, my discovery of how all the teachings I had received fit together was only really interesting as part of my own personal journey. I was thrilled to have a deeper understanding of the path I had been traveling for so long. A few months later, however, I realized I needed to create a course that would allow others to experience the life-development and consciousness work brought about by experiencing the elements. I was able to put to use in that course what I had so recently learned. Since that time, I have worked actively with the elements and shared what I know about them with others through my workshops, processes, audio books, and an oracle. The elements continue to teach me, and to bring me my next lesson as soon as I have integrated the previous one.

In the last few years, I have learned that the elemental forces served as the basis for the work of the ancient alchemists. Indeed, many of the ancient alchemists' hearts and minds were devoted to the work of personal transformation and of functioning at the highest level of consciousness. They studied and worked in harmony with the natural world. Proof of this lies in their drawings, which show their relationship with the sun, moon, stars, and elements.

I knew the priestesses of old also worked with the natural world, but I recently discovered how much of that work involved dance. The priestesses danced to unify heaven and earth, spirit and matter, and to infuse the physical world with the refined energy of spirit. Their dances represented the movements of the planets and the stars as they kept the sacred time and honored the natural rhythms of the physical world.

As my awareness and comprehension of these connected layers continued to unfold, I was struck by a new realization: I first learned to dance in my physical body to earthly music. Later, when I integrated expressive dance and activated the priestess within I learned to move my Spirit-filled-essence-self to the natural rhythm of celestial music. Spirit moved through me, the dancing priestess, and I became a living bridge into the world of matter. Here I am, full circle years later, with spirituality and the physical realm connected through dance to the natural world, much more than I ever thought possible.

There is much to share about how all the elemental and natural forces create the rhythms that move and flow within your life, expanding your consciousness and your capacity to co-create your life. Developing the coordination to co-create effectively, evolve your consciousness, or dance gracefully all progress, step by step, unfolding like the flower of life, petal by petal.

As you work with the material in this book, you do not need to be a dancer to understand any of it; just allow yourself to be open to dancing when the energy needs to move through you. You do not have to understand all the different energies I will be discussing at once either; just be open to what is new and moving in you at any moment.

This book is meant as a guide to the dance that is danced to the natural rhythms of the universe... the dance of life.

Blessings on your journey, *Lisa*

CHAPTER ONE

Dance of Creation

"There is a vitality, a life force, an energy, a quickening that is translated through you into action; and because there is only one of you in all time, this expression is unique. If you block it, it will never exist through any other medium and it will be lost. The world will not have it. You must keep that channel open. It is not for you to determine how good it is, nor how valuable, nor how it compares with other expressions. It is for you to keep it yours, clearly and directly."

Martha Graham

*Y*ou can learn ballet by coming into the classroom and just doing the steps, but you will understand and learn this form of dance much more easily if you actually have seen a performance. If you've watched a ballet, you will have a reference point. Then, when you come into class, you and your teacher can talk effectively about the lines dancers make in space, and how their arms and legs need to be held in order to have the energy move all the way through their bodies. And when you do the steps yourself and move your body into different positions, you will know how your physical form is supposed to look. If you haven't seen a performance, if you haven't seen how the dancers move and hold themselves, then the conversations with your teacher will have no context and the learning and understanding could come more slowly.

So, I am going to share the story and the pictures of what I call the "natural rhythms" with you first, to provide the visual reference point, as a ballet would for a dancer. On the written page, stories and illustrations seem to be the closest things to an actual live experience of the subject at hand. After that, we will come back to work with all the parts I have described and learn why each of them is important to you and the dance of your life.

The telling of any story can be done in many ways. Often many different versions of the same story exist. The perspective of the storyteller and the perspective of the one hearing the story each impact the story as well. When it comes to this particular story, it is not for me to determine if the story is good or has value. I simply offer it to you as one of the expressions of Spirit moving through me. As you read it, please notice how the story feels to you. Then feel free to use the parts of the story that work for your development at this time, and simply set aside the rest.

People familiar with the natural rhythm energies of the earth, sun, moon, and stars may feel they turn or flow in a different way. Some put the elemental archetypes in other directions. Regardless of where or how you place them, they all have lessons and energies to share. I have located the energies based on the Northern Hemisphere where I live. Placement may need to be different depending on the part of the world you live in. Allow your own inner wisdom to guide you to discover which energies you would like to work with and when.

The story I am about to tell you evolved out of my years of facilitation with presenting these concepts in classes. In my various workshops, I lay out several presentations on the floor using an Accelerated Learning format. As mentioned in the Introduction, Accelerated Learning is a teaching and facilitation method which engages the student in the learning process in ways they can more easily and immediately integrate and access the subject matter. Over the years, I realized how these separate presentations were more deeply connected to each other than I had previously known. That's when this story evolved and came to life before my eyes.

So settle in. Center yourself for a moment by taking a deep breath, and let the story begin...

Once upon a blue fold time...

in the dark center of the void, a quiet and subtle hum vibrated across the waters of the cosmos, and movement began. The substance that stirred in the time before time began its gentle sway, to and fro.

The source energy continued its movement, until two separate but connected energies emerged, an inward flowing receptive energy (yin-dark) and an active outer moving energy (yang-light). They loved dancing together and they stayed close in their movement for as long as they could evolve in that manner.

When they reached the end of their capacity to move together, they separated

—making room for each to grow and express. They chose in their separation to stay as connected as possible by taking both the energies of yin and yang with them. In their separation, the polarities of masculine and feminine were created. After their division, they decided that any future separation and expansion would always include both the energies previously expressed. Later these two energies would be called Great Mother and Holy Father, Goddess and God, Divine Feminine and Divine Masculine as well as many other names, yet both retained the yin and yang energies. Each took certain jobs in creation. The Divine Masculine brought forth his distinct function, his yin and yang expression, and proclaimed, "My masculine yin energy creates the seeds of any creation. I contain and protect the seeds until they are ready for sowing and planting. I hold the seedling energy until my masculine yang time comes to expand, penetrate, and ejaculate the seeds for planting. I use my yang masculine, goal-oriented energy to help bring any endeavor into focus and completion."[1]

The Divine Feminine declared her receptive and active expression in creation, and stated, "As the feminine receptive yin energy, I open to receive the seed and then to nurture and gestate it until the right time for its birth into the outer world of form.

I then ride the wave of the organic timing of my feminine yang energy so I know when to birth the creation. At the right time, I mightily push forth that new life from my nurturing womb space in which it grew."[2]

They sang the song of their love while dancing across the cosmos, and universes were born from their great union.

As they had agreed, all their creations contained the essence of the energies from which they were created. Each creation had at its core receptive and active qualities and carried with it the essence of its divine nature.

Out of the Divine Feminine and Divine Masculine's deep love for each other, our physical world was born. As this world moved into form, four fundamental energetic forces -- Earth, Water, Air, and Fire -- were birthed to hold its creational matrix. They were known from that time on as the elements or Elemental Forces and they agreed to work together to hold our world in form. After their birth, the Elemental Forces sat in council together and discussed the best way to shape the container of our world. They determined that they would work together as a unified field, with each having their own function and job.

The elements chose to become nature's foundation, and to express themselves as archetypal energies. They agreed to carry their archetypal energies in all expressions, even though their states would vary. For example, the element of Fire established that he would bring warmth and heat whether he shows up as the sun, a candle flame, a roaring fire, a chili pepper, or warm food heated on the stove. Each element felt the uniqueness of its expression and the great importance of working together with the other elements. Since they held the creational matrix of this world together, the elements decided they would gladly share their wisdom both individually and collectively with any future creations that wanted to learn and to grow from their knowledge.

To keep the matrix in balance, it was agreed that two of the four forces would carry a more feminine essence and the other two a more masculine energy. They also established that they would all carry both receptive and active qualities as well. Additionally, the Elemental Forces chose that their work together as a unified field would be accomplished in the same vibrational pattern that began the dance of creation – the yin and yang. They created that sacred light-dark pattern of balance as they positioned themselves in the four directions and established the solstice and equinox points.

As they came forth and moved into position, each force expressed its function in creation...

Earth spoke with solid groundedness when she took her place. "I am Earth, the physical realm of matter and your physical body. I create structure and form. My yin/yang expression shows in the need for rest and activity, my fallow and growing seasons, and the process of death and birth. According to the great wheel in the Northern Hemisphere, I take my home in the North and in the time when the greatest darkness gives birth to the light at Winter Solstice."

A river of words flowed from *Water* as she moved into position. "I am Water, the emotional realm. I run through the bloodstream as the rivers run across the earth. My yin/yang energies are connected to the cycles of the moon. My rhythm dances the tides in and out from the shore and sways your feelings from calm to intense. I take my home in the South, at the time of the greatest light, Summer Solstice. With Earth, together we form the feminine elemental axis – Earth contains me with her banks and shorelines and physical bodies and I nurture her. Together we connect to the deep inner terrain of beingness."

*Air* bellowed with a huge gust of wind as he found his location. "I am Air, the mental, vibrational and archetypal realm. I am the ability to think and to perceive the world. I work with the movement of the stars and the planets, bringing forth astrology and round table consciousness. My yin/yang movement is the breath going in and out of the body and the dance of vibration and sound. I take my home in the West, the balance point of light and dark, and the time of the Autumnal Equinox. I connect with Fire to form the masculine axis of the mental and the action realms, which are connected to the outer world of doing."

Fire heatedly expressed himself as he moved into place. "I am Fire, the action realm and the light realm. I am the life force that warms the earth and the crops for growth. I create the excitement and energy for any endeavor, and I am the spark needed to activate desire. I am the solar force, and I show my yin/yang expression in the turning of day into night and night into day. I take my home in the East at the Spring Equinox, one of the balance points of light and dark. At my time of year, the active growing cycle begins."

In their council meeting, they determined that the equal arm cross with a circle around it would be a symbolic reminder of how they hold our world in form.

The circle represents our world and the cross represents the four elements, the four directions (North, South, East, and West), and the four seasonal points.

The four seasonal points - the two solstices and two equinoxes - contained their own energies as well - and began a cyclic rotation perceived as time. The movement through all the solstice and equinox points is called "the turning of The Wheel of the Year," and with each full cycle another year passes and a new one begins. At Winter Solstice, the light is birthed from darkness for the new cycle and it grows until it reaches its height at Summer Solstice. It then begins the subtle movement back into the darkness. The equinoxes mark the complete balance points of light and dark that the wheel passes through each spring and autumn. Standing in their places they honored one another, as well as their unified energies that combine to hold this world in form.

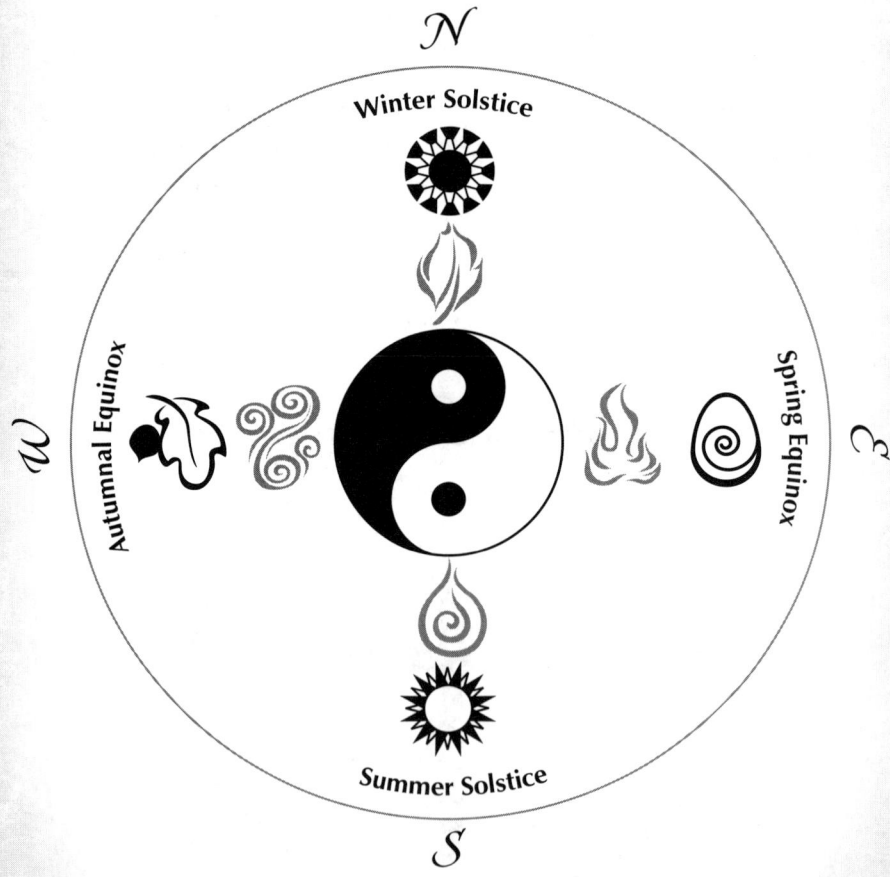

The solstices and equinoxes then began to notice the point halfway between each, when the energies started to turn toward the next season. Thus, they

began to honor those points and their energetic portals. They called them the "cross-quarter days." Each cross-quarter day marked the start of the energy for the new season, while the solstice or equinox days marked the height of that energy.

The cross-quarter days each gave voice to their energy as they stepped into place…

"I am the cross-quarter day of **Samhain**, also known as Halloween. I am both the ending point of the old year and the starting point for the next turning of the great wheel. I stand between Autumnal Equinox and the birthing of the light for the new growing cycle at Winter Solstice. From this point, I connect easily to the past and to the future as I stand between the two. Here the veil between the worlds, of what has gone before and what will come next, is the thinnest. I start the turning toward winter, with Winter Solstice being its fullest point. Harvest festivals will mark this time of year and mine will be the last. It will honor the old growing cycle before the beginning of the dark germination period prior to the next cycle. I can be celebrated at this mid-point, on October 31st."

"I am **Imbolc**, also called Brighid's day or Candlemas by some, and I come between Winter Solstice and Spring Equinox. I start the journey toward spring as the seeds begin to warm and stir from their slumber with the growing light. I bring the start of new life as the sun begins to gently heat the sweet earth. I am a time of creativity, purification, and regeneration. I provide a good opportunity for initiations or beginning any creative endeavor. I shall be celebrated on February first or second each year."

"I am **Beltane**, also known as May Day. I mark the point between Spring Equinox and Summer Solstice and begin the turning toward summer. I am the time of the year when we shall celebrate the union of the Goddess and God, the great sacred marriage. The sun is actively heating up the earth now, and their union creates the fertility for an abundant growing season. Performing ceremonies at this time will help to ensure the fertility of the land. I shall be celebrated on May 1st, halfway round the wheel from Samhain."

*"I am **Lughnasad** or Lammas. I shall be celebrated as the first of three harvest festivals beginning the quiet turn toward fall. I come at the mid-way point between Summer Solstice and Autumnal Equinox and can be celebrated on August 1st or 2nd. Just as grain will now be harvested, transformed into bread and then used as fuel for the body, harvest and transformation are the core teachings of my time of year. I stand halfway around the year from Imbolc. The energy that stirred then ripens now."*

All four of the solstice and equinox points, along with the four cross-quarter days formed the eight points of the Wheel of the Year. When all the points of the Wheel met together for the first time, they decided that they each would be one of the great teachers of change. The turning from point to point happened approximately every six weeks, thus naturally keeping the energy of change constantly in motion. The points determined this would teach those who work with them to learn to honor the cycles and rhythms of change and motion. The

Wheel of the Year provided a wonderful organic teacher of the natural process of life and death. Since the Wheel of the Year formed over the course of a year through the relationship of the earth and the sun, it was decided that Earth would claim the Wheel as one of her teachings.

Water decided that, since the moon had such a pull on her rhythms, she would take the monthly cycle it creates as one of her teachings. The moon makes the same yin/yang pattern in its journey each month that the sun makes with the Wheel of the Year as it grows and recedes. "For those attuned to the workings of these energies," Water said, "working with the moon will create a shorter rhythm of expansion and release for manifestation and creation."

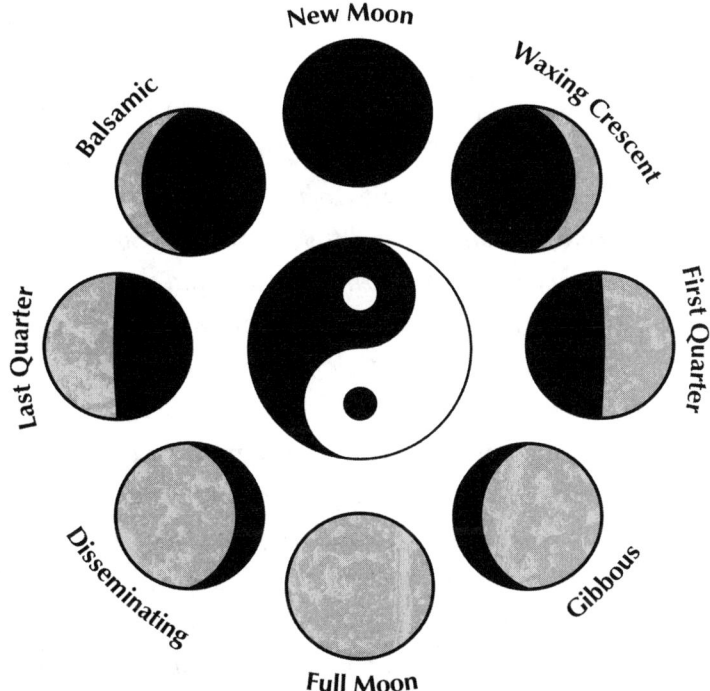

Water continued, "Working with the Wheel of the Year and the moon will teach the fundamental connection to the balanced energies of the yin/yang. The sun and moon create an alignment with the natural rhythms that move expression outwardly in the world and then turn naturally within to recharge, to reflect, to renew, and to bring forth new creations. Each of the special energies around the eight points of the Wheel of the Year or the sacred moon dance have a message and a teaching about change, transformation, releasing what is no

longer needed, and preparing for what is next. They shall also help those who work with them to know the sacred time or natural rhythm for doing something in their lives, which will help them line up with the natural flow of energy instead of working against it."

Air then suggested to the group an additional division of archetypal energies that both the sun and the moon could move through each month and year. He explained, "If the elements are sub-divided by three, they could create twelve astrological gates of awareness."

"These twelve gates of awareness would teach those who worked with them to have "round table consciousness." By passing through these gates with conscious attention, the archetypes would teach people who acknowledge them to achieve a large enough perspective on life to honor all twelve viewpoints, and all the ways in which those viewpoints might be combined."

"This would be my teaching," Air said, "as I am the one who brings the capacity to see things from all sides. Working with these astrologically related archetypes would allow different energies to better understand one another. They could learn to have compassion for the different ways things in this world need to be experienced. Thus, everything in this world would have an inner knowing of the twelve archetypal energies and would experience them during the course of each year as the sun passes through them and each month as the moon moves through each energy."

Air began giving directions to the elements to move into their three different archetypal expressions: "Fire, please place your energy in the archetypes of Aries, Leo, and Sagittarius. Water, be so kind as to move your energy into Cancer, Scorpio, and Pisces. Earth, please send yours into Taurus, Virgo, and Capricorn. And I will move into Gemini, Libra and Aquarius. These divisions will make it easier for others to understand some of our energetic subtleties," Air explained. The other elements thought Air's idea expanded the teachings in a beautiful way, so they divided into the archetypes as he suggested.

Air continued directing the others. "Let's have the masculine axis start the energy off here, since it is our turn next to express. Also, one astrological archetype associated with each of the four elements needs to fall directly in alignment with The Wheel of the Year, and we can call these Cardinal Points. Fire, why don't you start by positioning your first archetype of Aries at Spring Equinox. Cancer can take the Water point at Summer Solstice. Libra will take my Air point at Autumnal Equinox, and Capricorn can go into the Earth

position at Winter Solstice. As we position ourselves around the wheel, we will place ourselves in this order -- Fire, Earth, Air, Water -- that way we will have a masculine archetype followed by a feminine archetype, all the way around." The archetypes took their places on the wheel.

Once in place, the first group that Air assigned to the elemental astrological archetypes talked among themselves and decided to work personally with their element, through their individual experience of the particular element

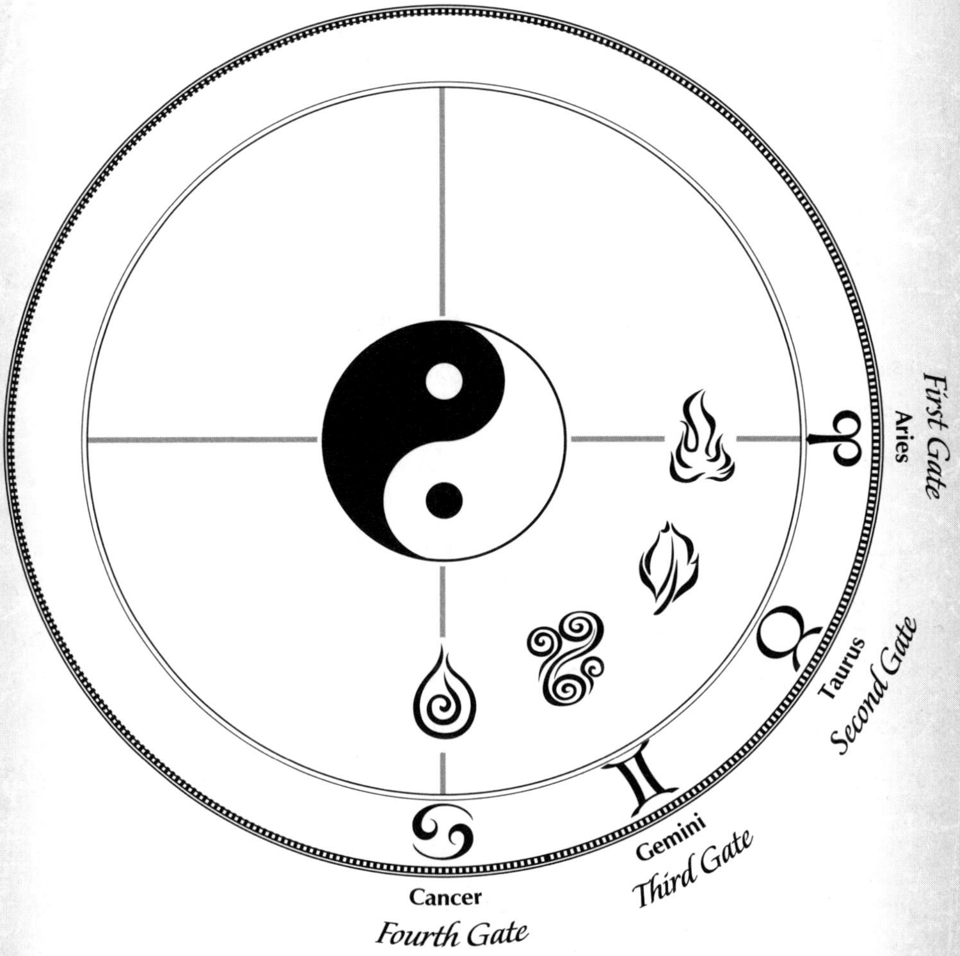

The First Four Gates of Awareness

First Gate
Aries

Second Gate
Taurus

Third Gate
Gemini

Fourth Gate
Cancer

influencing them. They would notice their constant relationship to their primary element, and so began to speak about themselves from this perspective...[3]

"I am **Aries**, a fire sign. I create the first gate of awareness, through which I teach the meaning of individuation. I am active, high spirited, and energetic. I love excitement, adventure, play, and competition. As a sacred warrior, I will fight to defend my beliefs and protect what I value in life. I like to go first, birth the new, get something started, and lead the way. I am courageous, trusting, decisive, inspired, and spontaneous. I am the Fire point of the cross at Spring Equinox."

"I am **Taurus**, an earth sign. I create the second gate of awareness, through which I teach the importance of enjoying the earthly realm of matter. I delight in all that looks beautiful, tastes delicious, and feels pleasurable. I love receiving the exquisite things and gratifications the physical realm has to offer. I also know how to take solid steps to fulfill my desires for possessions, wealth, and security. I connect to the Divine when I savor and enjoy intimacy through my body."

"I am **Gemini**, an air sign. I create the third gate of awareness, through which I teach the importance of the mind and ideas. I crave fresh experiences, change, fun, games, and imagination. I am versatile and curious and often play the comedian and perpetual youth. I am self-expressive through writing, speaking, or connecting to the divine muse through my many creative pursuits. I like to communicate, network, and bring news and information."

"I am **Cancer**, a water sign. I create the fourth gate of awareness, through which I teach the meaning of nurturing. I am the devoted caregiver to my family, friends, and projects. I love my home and comfort in all aspects of my life. I connect to those around me much like the loyal and caring mother/father. I am sympathetic to the vulnerability of others, and I create safe emotional space for what is tender, young, and growing. I am the water point of the cross at Summer Solstice."

The next group of the astrological archetypes decided their work with the elemental energies would expand to the next level. They would notice what happens when they express their particular elemental energy in relation to the world around them.

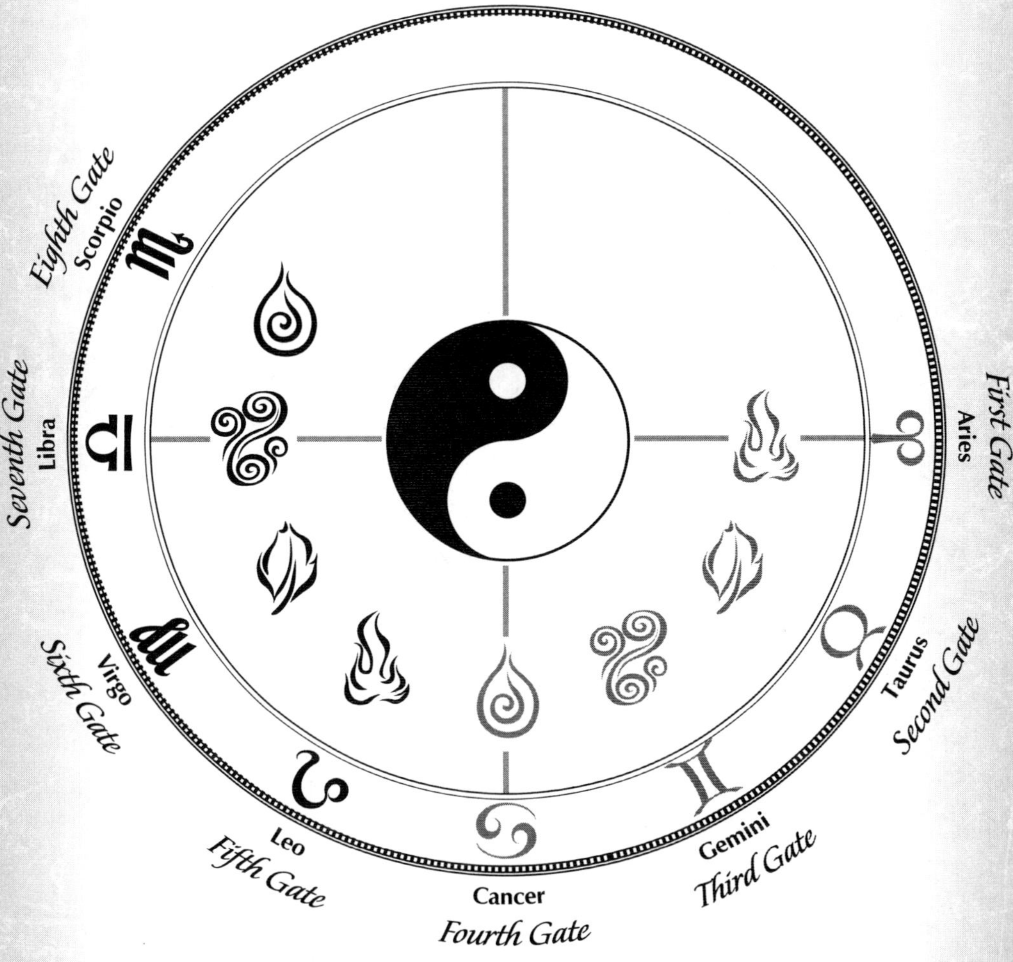

The Second Four Gates of Awareness

"*I am **Leo**, a fire sign. I create the fifth gate of awareness, through which I teach the value of radiance. I use the key of self-love to turn up my light and the brighter I radiate the more I inspire others. I am a natural leader, performer, star, director, and celebrity. I am self-confident, dramatic, regal, open-hearted, generous, creative, expansive, powerful, and outgoing. I love to be center-stage, a leading player celebrating and sharing my zest for life.*"

"*I am **Virgo**, an earth sign. I create the sixth gate of awareness, through which I teach the significance of dedicated work. I understand and honor patterns, timings, rhythms, and cycles. I access the Priest/ess within me to honor the sacred in the natural world through ceremony and ritual. I am organized, practical, dependable, productive, and a hard worker with a tremendous capacity for handling the details of the earthly realm. I am committed to doing my sacred work by being in service to the world around me.*"

"*I am **Libra**, an air sign. I create the seventh gate of awareness, through which I teach the importance of balanced relationships. I have the capacity to see things from all sides, honor each person's point of view, balance opposites, consider options and mediate well. I create safe space for all the gates of awareness to be valued. My cooperative social skills make me a good partner, hostess, and companion. Relationship is my spiritual path. I am the Air point of the cross at Autumnal Equinox.*"

"*I am **Scorpio**, a water sign. I create the eighth gate of awareness, where I teach the power of feelings. I fully experience the complete range of feelings, from icy and frozen to hot and steamy, and everything in-between. My training is to learn to master my response to them. I am intense and passionate about discovering what lies well beneath the surface of current awareness. I travel deep into my feeling waters to connect to source, and use the treasures I discover there to generate life force in myself and in others. I possess a potent intuition, or six-sense, and an ability to travel into other realms of consciousness.*"

The third division of the astrological archetypes decided their connection to their primary element would be at its most expanded state. They would connect to the collective, the world tribe, all of humanity, and even to the cosmos through their elemental energy.

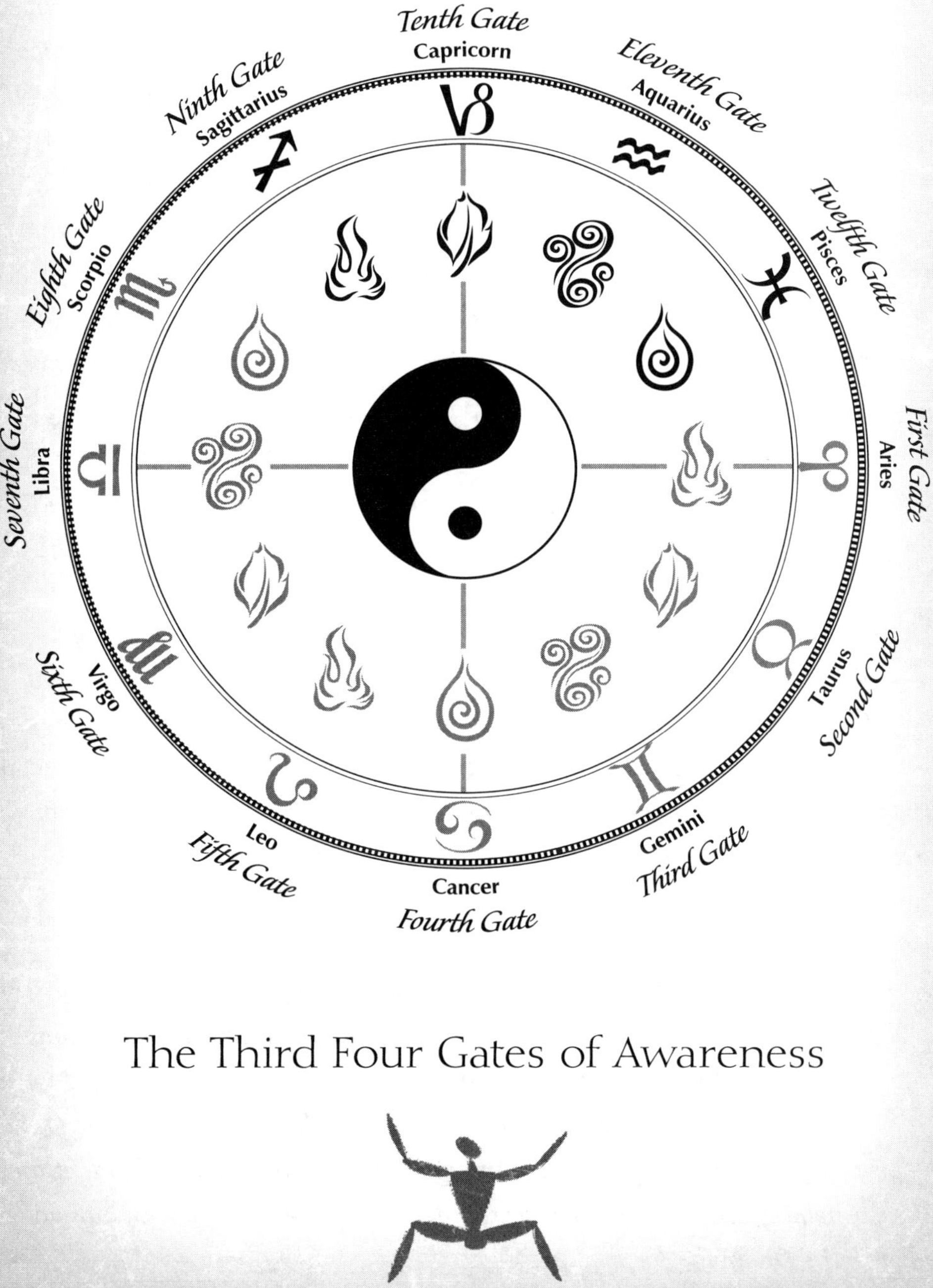

Tenth Gate
Capricorn

Ninth Gate
Sagittarius

Eleventh Gate
Aquarius

Eighth Gate
Scorpio

Twelfth Gate
Pisces

Seventh Gate
Libra

First Gate
Aries

Sixth Gate
Virgo

Taurus
Second Gate

Leo
Fifth Gate

Gemini
Third Gate

Cancer
Fourth Gate

The Third Four Gates of Awareness

"I am *Sagittarius*, a fire sign. I create the ninth gate of awareness, through which I teach the significance of expansion. I am the dynamic, outgoing, truth-seeking explorer. I constantly quest for expansion by physically and energetically seeking out new ideas and territories. I bring my expanded awareness and discoveries back to share with others as a teacher of philosophy and of evolving states of consciousness. I passionately search for the meaning of life through freedom, growth, and development."

"I am *Capricorn*, an earth sign. I create the tenth gate of awareness, through which I teach the value of structure and form. I am the administrator, the mature and wise one, the disciplined teacher, the hard working leader, the good provider, and the practical business person. I am ambitious, responsible, effective, efficient and goal-oriented as I bring new structures into earthly form. I create organizations and systems designed to last and support the generations to come. I am the Earth point of the cross at Winter Solstice."

"I am *Aquarius*, an air sign. I create the eleventh gate of awareness, through which I teach the importance of innovation. I have a cosmic perspective on life and often bring radical new ideas to humanity. I am the detached, free-spirited visionary exploring unconventional territory. I am interested in helping the world become a better place through humanitarian ideals of love and truth. I am unique, inventive, progressive, and original."

"I am *Pisces*, a water sign. I create the twelfth gate of awareness, through which I teach the importance of a compassionate heart. I feel the grief and suffering of humanity and respond with a loving caring heart that heals. I am deeply spiritual, intuitive, and psychic. I serve the world by dreaming the visions of a peaceful planet and selflessly helping others to create a better life. I completely merge with humanity and with the Divine."

After each of the elemental archetypes had spoken, they stood together in their respective positions on the circle. Based on those positions, they realized that when each of the same elemental energies joined, a triangle pattern formed.

Connecting the Earth Points

When both of the feminine elemental triangles joined together (the earth signs and the water signs) they formed a six-pointed star.

The Feminine Star

When the masculine elemental triangles joined, they formed another six-pointed star.

The Masculine Star

As the archetypes discussed their discoveries, they decided to have the six-pointed star be a symbol of balance and union, a reminder of Source from which we all spring.

They went on to connect both six-pointed stars to create a twelve-pointed star; they claimed it as a symbol for round-table consciousness.

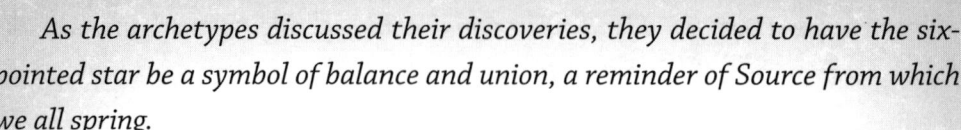

The Twelve-Pointed Star

As they all expressed their excitement over the discovery of the twelve-pointed star, Fire expressed an interest in adding his fundamental teaching into the mix. He said, "Earth, you work with the yearly cycle, and Water, you work with the monthly cycle. Air you add the twelve astrological gates of awareness to supplement an integrate both cycles. I want to work with the daily cycle. We will divide the day into twenty-four hours, and I will illuminate half of that time. This will serve as a reminder of the need for balance every day. We will have night and day, a dark time and a light time each daily cycle."

"I will also create two energetic portals each day," Fire continued. "One as I change from day to night - dusk, and one when I change from night to day - dawn. These portals will be powerful times to work with both the energies of day and of night and of the sun and of the moon. These portals will serve an especially important role when extra energy is needed for creational work."

He became extremely excited as he shared his next idea. "We can all work together at our best times to help those who will live on this planet to manifest their own creations effectively. When I am in my dawn or dusk phase, Earth is in a Wheel of the Year point (solstice, equinox or cross-quarter day), and Water is in its new or full moon cycle, together we can add extra energy or creational support to desires ready to come into form. The astrological archetypal energy that Air may be in at any given time will work especially well in these efforts. These will be powerful times to do ceremony on the planet."

They were all amazed at this wonderful idea of an even more powerful way in which they could work together. They loved thinking up new ways to create a beautiful and peaceful world of form in which balanced lives may be lived.

Eager to get started, they lined up together for the first time and began their work. Later they asked the planets and stars to join them in their duties. What fun they all had working in harmony. They even created beautiful celestial music as they moved together, which they called the music of the spheres.

As the energies continued to expand and to express, beings designed to play with the creational energies came into this world of form. The first people loved to play with creation and to honor the elemental energies. Then came the time of Great Forgetting, when the people of Earth no longer honored their deep connection to nature.

Many cycles later, after mankind had lost its connection with the energies of creation and the elements, people told stories of how the ancient and indigenous

people of the planet had been attuned with those very same energies. The tales described how people had worked with the powerful forces consciously and respectfully, and how they had understood the value of harmony and alignment with the energies forming the very core of creation. They had known that the fundamental forces of the world deeply appreciate those who honor and respectfully connect with them and they are eager to share when the people want to listen and to learn from their deep wisdom.

A few people somehow carried their connection to the elemental energies through the Time of the Great Forgetting. Then, during the Period of Remembering, these individuals shared with others what they knew: the forces of nature serve as our teachers and assist anyone who chooses to dance their life and their creations in time to the natural rhythms of the universe.

CHAPTER TWO

Fundamental Forces

"Dance is the only art of which we ourselves

are the stuff of which it is made."

Ted Shawn,
Time Magazine, 25 July 1955

$\mathcal{W}$e receive a powerful gift when we learn from the forces of nature. They have so much to teach us when we open to hear their wisdom.

Balance lies at the core of creation. Just as they did at the beginning, the receptive and active energies - yin and yang - constantly move in their sacred dance, from inside out and outside in. We can learn to sense this dance at work and at play in our lives. In fact, if we tune ourselves to hear the energies of nature, we find the forces of creation constantly communicating with us. They share their lessons and mysteries, assisting us to access a deep inner knowing that previously resided only in our unconscious mind or beyond our awareness.

Nature exists in a constant state of creating and letting go, and we follow suit. Consciously or unconsciously, choice by choice, we continuously create anew in our lives while releasing what no longer serves us. We do this not just with our minds but also with our hearts, bodies, actions, souls, and spirits.

Each outer force in nature corresponds to an internal energy, and they function in our consciousness and in our lives in much the same way they hold the outer world in form. Earth guides and informs us in the physical realm, Water in the feeling-emotional realm, Air in the mental realm, Fire in the action realm, and Spirit in our connection to the essence that flows through all things.

Together the elements of Earth, Water, Air, Fire, and Spirit weave the fabric of our world together, while actively functioning as teachers of consciousness. Each element teaches us from their outer world expression, as well as from how they work in our inner world. The more we become attuned to all the energies we work with, and that work with us, the clearer we can become about what we bring forth in life, and about how we respond to what comes to us. We learn to both receive external events outside of our control from a space of grace, love, and compassion and actively choose to direct our lives from a powerful internal position.

Learning from the forces of nature helps us to deepen our inner gifts and skills, as well as to express our increased co-creational abilities in the outer world. As we increase our awareness of the elements and begin working consciously with them, they assist us in understanding creation and manifestation, thus making a powerful difference in the quality of life we experience. Awakening to their underlying principles and teachings, we learn to become active co-creators of our own lives.

While learning to work with the energy of creation, we find ourselves going through the process of discovering different facets of who we are and how we function. To facilitate this process we need to become skilled at working with each element individually, and then practice aligning all of them together. We can consider each of the elements individually to discover each of their teachings. Ultimately they overlap and work with each other in so many interwoven and connected ways, that they can't be separated. Because of their inner connection, our proficiency at consciously aligning them in a unified field strengthens our capacity to bring forth our desires.

As our inner elemental teachers guide us toward growth, we find we will always have something new to understand or another skill to master. We must be patient with ourselves as we work with our current learning edges. Our capacity to work with the elemental energies and natural forces develops just as a child develops and learns new things, growing and changing and expanding in knowledge and ability over time. Processes take time, and we must allow ourselves the time to develop our awareness of and aptitude at working with the forces of nature. The rewards are well worth it.

Working with the Forces

To help you get the most out of the process of working with the forces, I recommend you keep a separate journal of your internal journey. Perhaps you can choose a journal that reminds you of the elements or of nature when you look at it. Also, you may find it helpful to create an altar to the elements in your home or office. This will help you honor and focus your awareness on them. In the chapter entitled "Elemental Tools," I offer some ideas about how to create your personal elemental altar. Remember these powerful forces appreciate and respond to your love, respect, reverence, and gratitude.

Spirit serves as our direct connection to the divine, flowing through each of us in a distinctive way. For this reason, we are all unique; no two beings are exactly alike. Each individual spiritual essence needs expression and to know that its full expression has value in the world. Without our expression of Spirit, a waits for our uniqueness to fill it. When we express our unique spirit and use our co-creational energy, we fill a void that is only ours to fill and we provide value to the world in the process.

When we work with the realm of Spirit we are working with the energy of Source as it existed before any distinction of energy. Everything simply was. As Spirit moved into the expressions of yin and yang, Spirit became known to some as Spirit and Soul. In this context, "Soul" represents the deep inner call or longing for our next level of growth, and "Spirit" represents the energy that connects us to and is the same as Source, or All That Is. In this book we will use "Spirit" to refer to the integrated energy of Source. When Spirit moves through an individual, it carries a desire for expression. That call to express is the essence of personal creation. However, often our desires for expression are larger than we can hold at a particular time, and when this happens, they compel us toward a new level of growth. This usually pushes us to our current learning edge and requires that we move past it into the terrain of new and greater knowledge and abilities. Working with the forces of nature, we accomplish this by learning to bring our desires from Spirit, align them with all the elements, and then anchor our creations on the physical realm of Earth.

Earth, the realm of matter, works with all the things that make up our physical life, our bodies, and the personal effects of our lives, such as our homes, cars, clothes, and finances, as well as our connected relationship to the physical planet itself.

Traditional Earth teachings train us to honor the earth, to honor the cycles and rhythms of nature, as well as to tune to our own cycles and rhythms. Too often in our modern culture, we follow only man-made cycles and mechanical time, becoming slaves to the calendar and to the clock. We need to remember to listen to the wisdom of our own bodies, of nature, and of our own deep sense of organic time, which work in natural unfoldment. When we follow rhythms out of harmony with our nature and our bodies, it can lead to stress or ill health. If however, we spend time in nature and synchronize with her rhythms, we will move deeply into our own nature, and the earth as well as our bodies become tremendous teachers, nourishing us in profound ways.

In fact, Earth teaches us to honor the physical and all aspects of life as sacred. From Earth we also learn the soul quality of gratitude, one of the highest vibrational energies available to us when we are creating our desires. When we are grateful for what we have, we open the energetic doorway for more abundance to flow into our lives. Earth also teaches us to elevate our lives through its gift of beauty. Looking at nature's beauty lifts our spirits.

Water flows through our lives keeping things supple, alive, and growing. Without water and its corresponding emotional realm, our nature can become dry, brittle, and hard like the ground without rain. We need the rich substance of our feelings to keep our life lush and growing.

The soul essence of love exists in the water realm. The clearer our emotions, the more space love has to move in our lives. In the emotional realm, we learn to love ourselves fully, to nurture and to heal our "inner child," the part of ourselves carrying the hurts, joys, and gifts of our early years of life. This creates a space for clarity, so love can move freely and fluidly in our relationships with others. Here we learn emotional maturity and discover better ways to care for ourselves emotionally, developing the ability to respond to instead of react to life and to others.

Water helps calm us and can lighten us up, making us more emotionally buoyant. The essence of Water centers or soothes us when we sit beside a river, stream, lake, or ocean, or soak in a bathtub or Jacuzzi. Water quenches our thirst and nourishes our essence.

Air, the mental realm, provides the medium through which sound and thought travel. Here the vibrational tone of our lives is set by the thoughts we think, how conscious we are of the spoken language we use, the integrated manner in which we use both the right and the left sides of our brains, and how we work with prayer, intention, and meditation. When we work in the vast realms of Air, we begin to see our lives from a larger perspective and to work with our visionary abilities. In Air we learn to soar, as we align our thoughts and personal energetic vibration in harmony with our life desires, enabling us to catch the wind beneath our wings and to fly.

Air and the mental realm also contain our belief systems about our lives. We have the ability to consciously choose our belief systems, although frequently much of their basis consists of outdated mental models or societal beliefs, passed down to us from our parents and grandparents, even though they no longer serve us. It takes dedication to change our belief systems and to consciously set a mental model for our lives.

Fire represents the action realm. Because of this element's volatile nature, people often express a fear of Fire getting out of control. Learning the skill of working with Fire requires focused and conscious training. During our lives, we are often taught to extinguish or to control our inner Fire -- our passion and our energy –- to sit still, be quiet, keep ourselves under control. Yet, in reaction to this enforced control, many people's fiery energy burns out of control. They rebel against the constraints placed upon them and move unconsciously toward extremes that exhaust their energy system. With the right type of training, we can learn to burn the flame of our lives at full force without burning ourselves out.

We can learn in this realm to be dynamic, to claim our personal power, to let our light shine brightly, and to feel passionate about life. When we possess too little Fire literally nothing happens in our lives. When we possess too much Fire, too much happens, and we burn out. Working with Fire requires balance and teaches us about balance itself. Fire also teaches us about the mysteries of transformation – literally, the changing of forms. Just as Fire changes whatever substance it burns, within us it facilitates the dying of an old part of the self, and its being born anew.

As we increase our ability to consciously work with the tools the elements offer, we increase our potential and effectiveness in life tremendously. Working with any one elemental energy improves our lives. Working with all of them and our lives become amazing! The teachings, principles and life-development tasks of each element provide us with the tools necessary for creating all that we desire, and for living in harmony with the twists and turns of life.

Please, honor and respect these amazing forces and guides, the elements. Remember to thank them for all they do to hold the world in form and for all they do for each of us personally. Our physical bodies serve as our containers for our personal connections to the elements. It is glorious that we possess the ability to move in our bodies, to feel the range of our emotions, to think, to perceive our world, to take action in our own lives, and to express our own unique spark of Spirit. Feel grateful for all these things, for gratitude is the song our souls sings to harmonize with Creation.

Whether you are new to working with the elemental forces or have had years of experience, you have the potential to awaken many new layers of consciousness as you work with this book. How deep you go and how much you learn depends upon you. For the elements to actually share their knowledge with you, they need your presence and your willingness to learn, and they will share with you if you simply approach them respectfully from a place of honoring and integrity, and ask to learn.

I urge you to keep an open mind and heart as you develop your own personal relationship with the Elemental Forces. You may have a different way of languaging your experience, or a contrasting mental model than the one presented here, or perhaps you have a belief system that seems to come from a different background. No set way to work with the forces exists. The elements function in all of us. They can and will work with you from your perspective if you invite them to do so. No matter from which direction you approach or from which perspective you look, you will find that nature contains amazing and powerful forces, and they sincerely appreciate you working with them.

Elemental Connection

*A*s you begin working with the elements, they like to introduce themselves so you can become familiar with the feeling of each of their essences.

To begin your personal work with the elements, allow yourself time to go outside in nature and connect with each one individually.

The following pages contain journaling exercises for each element. Space is provided in the book for your answers or you may choose to answer the questions in your personal elemental journal.

Begin by taking your book and your elemental journal or some blank paper and going outside to your favorite place in nature. Sit on the ground. If possible, go to a place near a body of water. If one is not available, do the journal exercise with water the next time you are in the bathtub or have just taken a shower.

When you get comfortable, open your journal and begin the sacred journey of deepening your connecting with the forces of nature.

 Spirit

Take time to feel, to touch, and to connect with the spark of Spirit that flows through all things. Allow your consciousness to feel the energy of Spirit and ask it to reveal its essence to you. Thank Spirit for the amazing gift of life.

Notes on Reflection with Spirit:

Personal Spirit Realm

Exercise for personal connection to Spirit :

In seated or in moving/dancing meditation, connect with the spark of Spirit that is you. Honor it as sacred. No other spark exists the same as you. Ask it to reveal to you a way or ways in which you can more deeply honor the spirit of your uniqueness in your life.

How well do you create in life?

Are there ways in which you now choose to create your life more powerfully?

How in tune do you feel with your life essence?

 Earth

Take time in nature to feel, to touch, and to connect with the element of Earth. Allow your awareness, your consciousness to sink deeply into the soil beneath you and deeper down into the earth's body. Ask the earth to reveal her essence to you. Then just wait and listen. When you receive a message, write down the message from Earth without filtering it. Remember to thank Earth for all that you receive from her bounty.

Notes on Reflection with Earth:

You are part of my body, like the trees, grass, & animals! You draw your life from me.

Solid, physical, 5 senses, Beauty, Life Force, Manifestation, grounding, Birth, growth, Abundance, Fertility, Body, Form

Personal Earth Realm

Exercise for personal connection to Earth:

In seated or moving/dancing meditation, connect with your physical body. Honor it as sacred. Thank it for all it does for you by containing your spirit in the world of form. Ask it to reveal to you the ways in which you can more deeply honor in your life the element of Earth.

→ Practice looking@ the trees until you can see their energy field.
→ Practice tasting energy

Do you need to adjust or balance the physical matter in your life, body, foundations, or finances in any way?

Are you grounded and taking solid steps toward your life desires?

Do you need to take more time for quiet and reflection to balance all the "doing" in your life?

How in tune do you feel with the element of Earth in your life?

 # *Water*

Take time in nature to feel, to touch, and to connect with the element of Water. Allow your consciousness, your awareness, to sink deeply into the water. Ask Water to reveal its essence to you. Then just wait and listen. When you receive a message, write down the message from Water without filtering it. Remember to thank Water for the rich substance it provides.

Notes on Reflection with Water:

Personal Water Realm

Exercise for personal connection to Water:

In seated or moving meditation, connect with the watery realm of your feelings and emotions. Honor them as sacred. Thank them for all they do for you. Are there areas of your life where you need to feel what is going on more deeply?

Are there ways in which you need to adjust or balance the water in your life, such as going more with the flow, or honoring your intuition?

Do you need to clear any emotional baggage by clearing up past relationships, etc.?

Are your emotions balanced?

Do you create space for your feelings?

How in tune do you feel with Water and the emotional realm in your life?

Air

Take time in nature to feel and to connect with the element of Air. Allow your awareness to merge with Air. Ask Air to reveal its essence to you. Then just wait and listen. When you receive a message, write the message from Air without filtering it. Remember to thank Air for all that you receive.

Notes on Reflection with Air:

Personal Air Realm

Exercise for personal connection to Air:

 In seated or moving/dancing meditation, connect with your breath. Ask Air to reveal to you the ways you can more deeply honor the element of Air in your life.

 Are you working with the mental realm and Air effectively, holding a positive vision for your life?

Are you using prayer, meditation, and intention to consciously set the tone of your life?

Do you feel a sense of freedom in your life?

How balanced is the exchange of giving and receiving in your life?

Fire

Take time in nature to connect with the element of Fire. To do so, use the sun, a candle, or build a fire. Allow your consciousness to connect with the fire. Ask Fire to reveal its essence to you. Then just wait and listen. When you receive a message, write down the message from Fire without filtering it. Remember to thank Fire for all that you receive from its essence.

Notes on Reflection with Fire:

Illumination, magic. Purification. Passion. Heat. Warmth. Nurture. Feed. Grow. Alchemy. Conjuring. Eater of Impurities. Shining your light. Brilliance. Showing the way. Creates/Illuminates Shadows. Cooking.

Clear womb space. Be discerning of where I ~~spent my time~~ + attention: esp. online. (Fire needs conscious Breath)

1 Clear + transform office
2 Templify Temple
3 Create plant marketing for Temple Retreats
4 Scan family photos
5 MudraSong Video
6 Wkly Transmissions
7. Google + etc.
8. Set elemental WB
9. Dance Daily
10. Connect !! Guides etc.

Personal Fire Realm

Exercise for personal connection to Fire:

In seated or moving meditation, connect with your life force. Honor it as sacred. Thank it for all it does for you to keep your life fired up and alive. Ask it to reveal to you the ways you can more deeply honor the element of Fire that is in your life.

Move · Dance · Rest · Eat Well
Detoxify physically & energetically
Shields · Boundaries

Are you passionate about your life or perhaps burning yourself out? Do you need to adjust or balance Fire in your life in any way?

We have a good balance,
now, I feel.

How are your vitality, sexuality, and sensuality?

A - Sensuality
C - Vitality
F - Sexuality

How easily do you handle the process of transformation?

With ease — I welcome it!

Are you in tune with Fire in your life?

more every day

Are you taking powerful action in the world?

Yes

General Reflections

What did you notice about how the elements felt in comparison to one another?

Were some elements easier to connect with than others?

With which elements do you feel you need the most work?

Did you hear their responses equally, or were one or two of them more difficult for you to connect with and to hear?

As you move forward with your elemental work, allow your increased awareness to guide you in your development with each of the Elemental Forces of Creation.

In the chapters ahead, Spirit and the elements will introduce you to each of their mystery school teachings. A mystery school is a body of knowledge that is said to be beyond full human understanding. To facilitate understanding, each element has multiple training paths that are designed to reveal more about itself and its mystery school lessons. People are drawn to a training because it works in harmony with their own energy. Notice which training path you are drawn to, and how it fits your unique energy. The elements also will share with you their key words and powers, as well as the soul qualities their training develops. Your important task revolves around beginning to understand and embody the element's fundamental teaching and doing the element's developmental task. Eventually you will have a strong conscious awareness and some degree of fluency in working with all of them.

If you perform the power activations suggested for each element, please note that those elemental powers will be awakened within you. You will, therefore, need to take additional responsibility for using them wisely. It is imperative that the elements and their energies be used for the highest and greatest good of all and never against anything or anyone. Your intention is vital to what you are creating and bringing forth in your personal life, as well as to the energy it adds to the human collective. It is time for each of us to claim our power as co-creators of our experience and to begin focusing our energies on our desired outcomes. To do so, let's begin in the next chapter with Earth to discover a deeper understanding of each of the elements and their mysteries.

CHAPTER THREE

Earth

"I see dance being used as communication between body and soul to express what is too deep to find words..."

Ruth St. Denis

Earth

Physical Realm

Mystery School Teachings:
Working with structure and form, earth-based spirituality, honoring the seasons and cycles, finance, beauty and aesthetics, body development, body knowing, body energy systems, nutrition, coordinated physical movement, sacred sites and more.

Developmental Task:
To Embody Wholeness

Key Word: Sacred

Soul Quality: Gratitude

Ecstatic Realm: Touch

Primary Power: To Stand on Your Own

Level 2 Power: Alignment

Natural Rhythm Cycle: Wheel of the Year

*T*he physical realm provides a container for our experiences here on Mother Earth. The earth itself is an amazing being. Look around. Go out in nature and explore earth's lakes, mountains, flowers, deserts, and jungles. Each varied face she presents in her natural state is filled with beauty. Earth provides our food and shelter and serves as the source for all our experiences of the material realm. And those earthly experiences bless us with abundant gifts.

The physical containers we know as our bodies allow each of us to have an individualized experience of life on earth. Our bodies hold our Water, Air, and Fire, along with the spark of Spirit that constitutes our individual essence. With the blessing of a physical container, our bodies, we are given the gift of being able to touch one another, to experience a kiss, to hold the hand of a child, to feel the sun on our face, to open to the magic of movement, to taste the ripeness of delicious fruit, and so many more earthly delights. When we are conscious of these gifts, we realize our bodies are a priceless miracle.

How often do we take the time to appreciate the rich and abundant blessings of the physical realm? When connected to the value of physical experience, we develop the soul quality of Earth, which is expressed as gratitude -- gratitude for every moment of health, for every time we wake up in a warm bed, have a full belly, hold another person, dance the night away, or walk in nature. Since we feel gratitude at the core of the soul, this emotion often is expressed in tears of appreciation.

The element of Earth teaches us to honor the physical realm: to live in a state of gratitude and grace, to be aware of cycles and transitions, to form an internal connection to the sacredness of our life, and to embody wholeness. It is here we also learn to work with discipline, structure, and form, and to appreciate the gifts that beauty brings to our life. Earth functions as our loving teacher and guide as we live and journey upon her, and exist upon her "body," and live within her containment in our personal Earth — in our own bodies. Connect to Earth's teachings, and remember to give thanks to the element of Earth and to honor the gifts of the physical realm.

Earth Skills and Powers

Earth's fundamental skill development is found in her capacity to structure and create form. It takes discipline to work with Earth -- to create form or to bring an idea into being. Whether we are organizing a home, writing a book, having a child, running a business, or maintaining a body, we need a certain amount of personal discipline and internal structure to take the idea of what we want to create from the mental and spiritual realms and bring it through all the layers of creation into full form in the earthly realm.

Earth teaches us to lay one brick at a time, take one step then the next, write the first chapter then the second, and work from the foundation up to complete anything in the physical realm. Even though the other elements can assist us in accelerating our accomplishments, when it comes to anchoring an idea on the earthly realm, it happens in steps and stages. That is the way matter forms. For example, a child in the womb begins with one simple cell division, which is followed by another and another until the child is developed completely. A healthy child's systems all develop at the correct phase. Earth teaches us about the organic growth and developmental process.

By forming our world through the organic growing process, we learn patience, trust, and discipline. In that process we also discover our own level of balance in the earthly realm. For instance, if we are not using Earth well, we can become ungrounded. We may have a lot of ideas but not get them anchored or into their full form. If we become too grounded, stuck in life and unable to move, we may have too much Earth.

When we have an abundance or a lack of an element, often we need to work with another element to help us balance the other. When we find ourselves ungrounded, we may need to focus more on Air to help us discipline ourselves enough to choose one idea at a time to ground and carry out to completion. If we are too grounded, we may need to explore Water to discover in what ways our emotions might be holding us in place, or perhaps, we need to add more Fire to our lives to liven things up a bit and get us moving.

As we learn and explore each elemental realm, we begin to discover which elemental energy we need to increase within ourselves to bring them all into a powerful state of balance and co-creation. We can liken this to tending a physical garden. Looking to the elemental forces as our guides, we can see in our "life garden" if we need more rain, sun, wind, or fertilizer. Through our ability to observe, we are reminded over and over again that we are an essential ingredient in our co-creations, and it is up to us to tend to the garden of our own lives. We are the ones responsible for how our garden is growing and how our lives are developing. All we need to learn is what to add next in order for us to thrive.

Earth's primary power lies in its capacity to form a physical container that allows each of us, as individual sparks of Spirit, to stand on our own. We need the earthen container of our bodies to function as separate, individuated beings. Like any individuated structure, our body provides us with the ability to stand whole and complete. As children, we spend all our early years learning to do just that. From simply standing on our own legs, to walking and running, to learning to stand independently in all areas of life.

With the gift of a body, we develop the ability to stand alone, complete and whole unto ourselves. Only after developing this inner power can we fully function with others in inter-dependent ways. This process teaches us how to bring forth our co-creations, and to discover how we influence and affect the world around us with the choices we make, the feelings we have, the thoughts and words we entertain and express, and the actions we take in life.

The earthly realm deeply responds to how it is treated. Every interaction we have with the physical world creates a response that tells us something about how we are engaged with it. If we ignore, judge, criticize, or otherwise mistreat the physical world, those kind of results appear in our lives. A falling down house, an overgrown garden, a body that shows years of abuse and mistreatment, finances that reflect our neglect, or a life that is filled with frustration all correlate to our relationship with Earth energy.

By coming to terms with the perfection of the earthly realm's response to how it is treated, as co-creators we can make sure to infuse our earthly realm with what it needs to shower us with blessings. We can take care to love and to impart the grace of divine thankfulness in our lives, being grateful for all we are given from the earthly realm.

We can learn to release anything in our lives with which we are no longer in right relationship, giving things we no longer need or want to someone else who will value and appreciate them. We can discover that our bodies truly thrive on our kind thoughts and treatment. We know the ways to treat our bodies well: clean air, pure water, time in nature, fresh food, and plenty of movement, laughter, gentle touch and words, and loving adornment. The body responds in kind by uplifting us, releasing its stress, and staying healthy and vibrant. We apply the determining factor here. We apply choice to what we co-create in our physical world.

Exercise: Clearing the Physical Realm

Do this exercise when you need upliftment or fresh energy in your life. Go through your closet, your home, your car, your garage, your files, your pantry, your photos, your attic and any other places you store things, one item at a time. Remember all those objects store energy. You can ask yourself with each item if the energy of that item is still meaningful for you or not. Ask if it is old and needs to be released. Weed out what you no longer need and release it to others by selling it or giving it away. Notice with each release how the energy of your life feels. Keep only objects that hold the energy of what you love and what you are choosing for your life now.

Just as our bodies respond to our loving, grateful treatment, so do our children, homes, cars, gardens, jobs, finances, wardrobes, and the earthly planet we live on. The people of Peru know this and have a beautiful tradition to thank and honor the Earth Mother, whom they call *Pachamama*. They create a blessing bundle for Earth called a *despacho*, which they give to her during ceremony, as a way of expressing gratitude for all the Earth Mother provides.[1] The *despacho* gives energy of upliftment back to her. A

Peruvian Shaman typically creates this bundle in Peru, but anyone can create a similar one and honor Earth in this way.

The blessing ceremony basically consists of making a little gratitude food pack for *Pachamama*. The Shaman spreads out some type of paper or biodegradable wrapping and then fills it with a variety of natural ingredients: sweet treats, cornmeal, tea, coca leaves, flowers, and the like. The Shaman says a prayer each time an item is placed on the paper, to bless the Earth Mother and give thanks for all she provides. When the beautiful creation is complete, it is wrapped up and tied. Then the *despacho* is either buried or burned. *Pachamama* feels the gratitude and honor placed in the *despacho* and sighs with delight at being appreciated. In a sacred way, the ritual raises the vibration of the entire area where the ceremony is held. Taking the time to do a *despacho* ceremony serves as an excellent way to honor the element of Earth.

We can find many ways to practice working with the element of Earth, from earth-based spirituality, honoring seasonal cycles, doing ceremony, becoming a priest or priestess, or expressing gratitude, to honoring more everyday things such as studying finance, uplifting the look of a home, planting a garden, reorganizing a wardrobe, or studying a body-development technique such as dance or a martial art form.

Remember, the energy we place or expend in the earthly realm creates the vibration around which the matter of our lives forms. Thus, understanding and being able to work with the element of Earth is essential. Earth provides the foundation for all the other elemental teachings, and all the other elemental energies work in relationship to Earth. Thus, we too, must achieve at least some level of mastery in working with Earth to move comfortably to more evolved levels of being.

Exercise: Forming Earth

Clay provides a wonderful way to practice forming and working with Earth. You may want to purchase some clay and create a sacred object for your altar. To create your altar piece with sacred intention, hold your desire in your heart and mind as you infuse prayers and blessings through your words and thoughts as you shape the clay. When you use your sacred intent to form an object, you infuse it with your prayers and blessings. Not only is working with clay fun to do, it serves as a wonderful practice to learn to form your life with sacredness and intention.

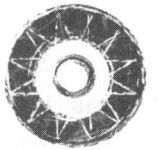

Activation: Earth's Primary Power to Stand on Your Own

Preferably do this exercise standing. If for any reason you cannot stand, your intention will work to activate the power while you remain seated. Find a piece of music that feels very strong, earthy, and grounded to you. Before listening to the music, state your intention out loud or in your head. State through intention that you want to activate Earth's energetic power to stand on your own as an individuated being. Place your awareness in your body, then play your music, and dance to activate, enliven, and embody your intention. Dance in any free-form way that feels powerful to you. Once complete with the dance, focus your awareness in your legs, and ask them what you need to know about standing on your own. Then listen internally, and journal the response.

Exercise: Planting Your Desires

The next time you plant seeds, flowers, shrubs, or trees do so with intention. State aloud or hold in your thoughts the desire(s) you choose to bring into being by planting. This will activate your intention. As you plant, hold within your body the feeling of that desire as already fulfilled. Give thanks for the power of Earth to ground your desires. If when watering the plant you are grateful again for the fulfillment of your desire, this adds additional "creation juice" to your desire .

Following the power to stand on our own, Earth next offers us the power of alignment. We gain access to this power as we align our physical bodies with the earthly and spiritual realms, and act as living bridges between heaven and earth. This alignment gives us the ability to infuse the physical realm with Spirit. We can bring this Divine energy into our physical bodies and the physical world only to the degree that our body container and consciousness are open to it and strong enough to hold the energy. Because certain archetypes already work in the spiritual realms, activating them within our consciousness can help us deepen our capacity to work with Divine energy. Aligning ourselves internally with such archetypes as the priestess, priest, shaman, sage, minister, and mystic open us further to the subtle spiritual realms and vibrations, and increase our capacity to run those energies in our physical bodies. The more we strengthen our earthly physical container, so it can hold and use the vibrations of divinity, the greater becomes our capacity to infuse Spirit into matter.

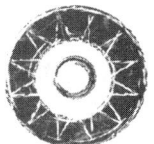 **Activation: Earth's Level Two Power of Alignment**
Do this activation after you have completed all level one primary-power elemental activations. Activate your awareness of this Earth power by taking a few minutes to stand or sit on the earth. Connect to your body and the power of its physical containment. Give thanks to your earthly body for housing your spirit. Now project your consciousness deep into the core of the earth and feel the connection to the Earth Mother. While keeping your consciousness in the center of the Earth, also with your intention project your consciousness into the center of the heavens, the Galactic Core. From this vantage point, ask your body to become a living bridge between heaven and earth. Open your body to receive an infusion of energy from both Spirit and matter simultaneously. This experience activates the level-two power of Earth: the power of alignment.

Earth's Developmental Task

Earth's developmental task requires us to embody wholeness and to embrace all aspects of life as sacred. Wholeness is a state of inclusiveness that encompasses all aspects of consciousness. Our bodies contain all the elemental energies, and without them we would be unable to have any experience on this physical plane of existence. The element of Earth contains our spirit, our essence, and gives shape and form to who and what we are physically. Since each element and its realm play an essential part in our capacity to function fully, when we honor each one of them for their sacred purpose, we perform our Earth developmental task of embodying wholeness.

Wholeness includes both our ability to separate and to function in a model of inclusion. In other words, we are not simply either whole or separate, light or dark, receptive or active, we are both...and. Our nature is one of wholeness, and we embody the capacity to separate, to work with both light and dark, to function in both receptive and active ways. We are Spirit and matter.

Separation, or individuation, functions as a developmental aspect of wholeness. We can separate the elemental forces one from another to explore them, work with them, understand them, and commune with them. Yet ultimately they cannot be separated. Can you separate earth from sky? Can you separate your breath from your body and still exist in this physical form? The elements are interconnected, and yet we find tremendous benefit in working with their separate characteristics to deepen our awareness of them. Learning from their individual aspects is very different from rejecting, denying, dismissing, or diminishing them.

In fact, rejection of any one part of the whole diminishes our capacity for a consciousness of wholeness. When we dismiss, deny, or deem inferior any one part of creation, it becomes more challenging to fully embrace all the other parts. This can lead to deep imbalance within ourselves and within our world. Many examples exist of the wounding this type of imbalanced energy can create. Past experience has shown us the damage that can be done, for instance, if one sex is considered superior to the other, or one skin color or religion is held as better than another.

The same is true when we value any one part of creation over the other. If the mental realm is considered better than the emotional world, then often an internal split between head and heart is created. To truly be effective in life and in alignment with all parts of ourselves, we need to value the wisdom of the head and heart.

The same holds true if the physical world is considered less than the spiritual world and its value diminished. We then may experience an internal separation of Spirit and matter. In the past this has lead much of humanity to disconnect from the Earth Mother. Culturally, we began treating the earth in ways that did not serve our own wholeness or the wholeness of the planet. As a result of humanity's energetic disconnection from the earth, many areas of our beautiful planet have been left stripped, barren, and environmentally imbalanced.

Spirit is continuously expressing in this world of form, and to have our spiritual experience in the physical realm we need both our earthen bodies and our beautiful planet. Only when we honor our planet and our bodies as sacred vessels can we begin to fully connect Spirit and matter. We need to remember the true value of the earthly realm, to care for our earthly home and the temple of our spirits — our bodies. As we honor matter in the form of all things physical, we perform the developmental task of Earth and embody wholeness. From this place of wholeness, we bring Spirit more fully into our bodies and our lives.

Through the changes of the seasons, as Wheel of the Year turns, Earth gives us a powerful model for understanding her developmental task. The Wheel of the Year helps us move through the cycles of light, dark, growth, death, and rebirth. As we understand the purpose and meaning of each phase in the cycle of change, we begin to fully embody wholeness.

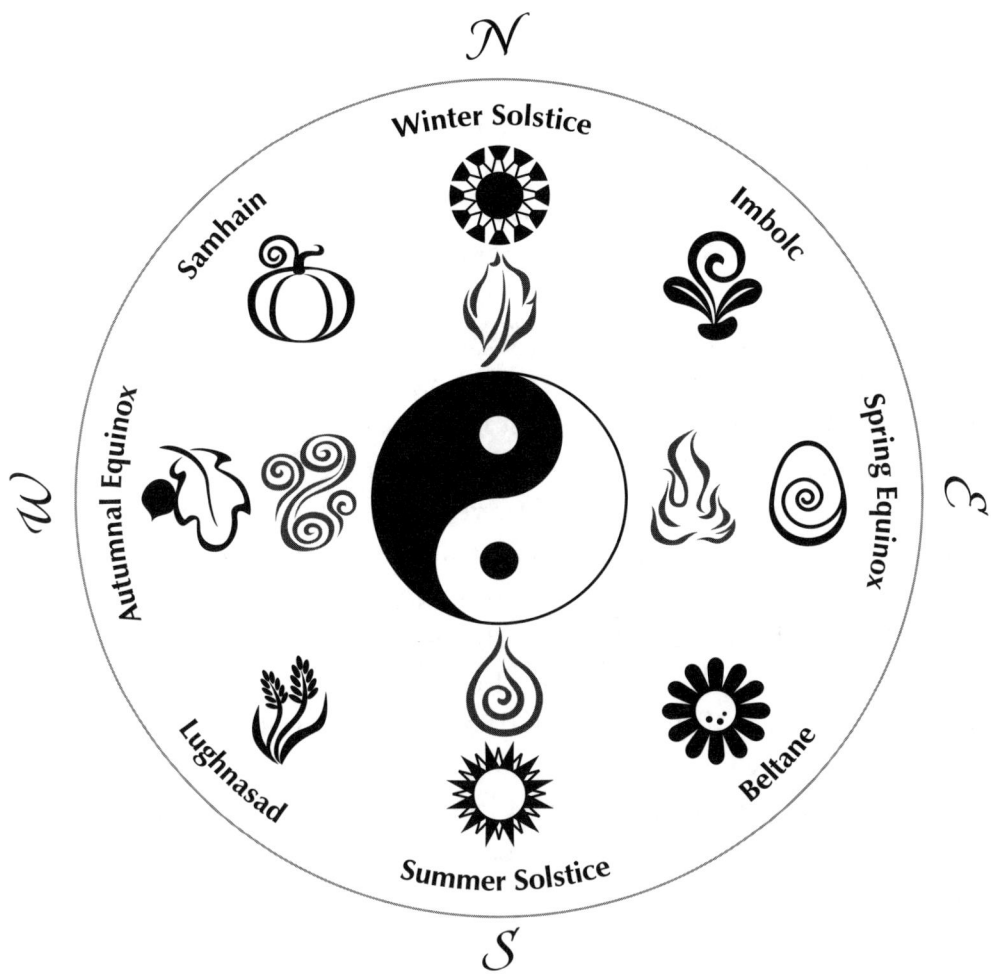

Natural Rhythm Cycle: Wheel of the Year

Each element possesses a natural rhythm cycle. Every day, every night, every month, and every year dances to a rhythm. The Wheel of the Year connects the sun's journey to the earth's cycles. In many cultural views of the Wheel of the Year, the sun was seen as carrying the masculine principle, called "Son" and "God", while the earth was viewed as the feminine principle, named "Mother Earth" or "Goddess." The Earth Goddess has many names, varying across cultures. In many myths, the relationship and connection of the Earth Goddess with the Solar God was honored with the changing cycles. The Earth Mother Goddess stays alive throughout the year, changing from mother, to partner, to sovereign Goddess. The solar, sun, (son) God energy is born from the Goddess, grows to full Godhood, becomes partners with the Goddess, and then dies each year. The Wheel teaches us the natural cycle of death and rebirth, as one year's cycle gives way to the next.

Through the seasonal Wheel of the Year, light and dark work as a harmonious whole. They constantly move together in a dance both sacred and essential to our well-being. Living in continual light would burn out our systems, because we would have no time of rest or quiet. Conversely, with too little light we would tend to get depressed. We need the balance of both light and dark to achieve a state of wholeness.

The same holds true in our inner world. The light time of our inner world is filled with doingness and activity, just as in the outer world. This busyness requires balance with beingness during the quiet rest in times of darkness. Our inner darkness serves as a void, a place where we are receptive to the inner voice of Spirit, and where seeds of our desires are planted, developed, and grown. In this place, we connect to All That Is and in the dark, rich, fertile soil new awareness grows to full expression.

The seasonal cycle reminds us of our need for balance through every turn of the Wheel of the Year's quarters: the winter and summer solstice points and spring and autumnal equinoxes. As those four sections divide again, creating the cross-quarter days, each of these eight points of seasonal change are a "power day." Each is honored and celebrated for the energy they bring to the year.[2]

Samhain, in the Northern Hemisphere, is the place on the Wheel of the Year where the yearly cycle both ends and begins anew. Samhain is celebrated on October 31st and is also called All Hallow's Eve or Halloween. It marks the final harvest for the growing cycle, the end of one year, and the reflection phase of the next turning of the Wheel. As the old passes away and a window opens for the new to enter, it is said that the veils between the worlds (the old and the new) become thin. Many people who honor the Wheel use this window as a time to honor the past and our ancestors, which explains the origins of Halloween costumes, which look like ghosts, and skeletons.

This power window represents a time to honor the harvest of the past year with thanks and gratitude, to give tribute to what has passed away, and to honor death as part of the natural cycle of life. Some say that on this day the sun dies and is seeded in the womb of the Goddess for rebirth. Thus, Samhain represents an opportunity to notice what needs to be released in our life and, perhaps, give away what is no longer needed.

At Samhain, we are entering the darkest days of the year, so during these few weeks we need to spend time turning within for the deep rejuvenation that the quiet stillness of darkness brings. As we do so, it is also important to notice what is stirring in our own inner realm. Notice the ideas and feelings that may want to come to light or be birthed during the next growing cycle. The window opened by this power day brings a wonderful opportunity to look at the signs and symbols showing up in our lives, for the coming year, through divination. Oracle readings, animal totems, or working with our favorite symbol system helps us gain access to these new cycle energies.

The cross-quarter days actually mark when one season begins to turn toward the next. As such, Samhain begins the turning toward winter, with Winter Solstice being the peak of that season.

Winter Solstice marks the place on the Wheel where the sun, which went deep into the dark space of the womb during Samhain, is reborn. We begin here with the gradual day-by-day increase in light until it reaches its peak at Summer Solstice and begins, once again, its turn toward the darkness. Winter Solstice, also known as Yule, typically falls between December 20 and 23 and is the shortest day and the longest night of the year.

Winter Solstice is seen as the time when the Goddess gives birth to the "sun," or "son," the masculine principle. The light of the sun emerges reborn out of the darkness year after year. Thus, traditionally we honored this point on the wheel by bringing evergreen trees into our homes to represent the everlasting nature of the Earth Goddess. They were decorated with images representing what we wanted to bring into our lives for the coming year. Gold balls represented the life force of the sun, icicles symbolized rain, paper money or coins stood for abundance, pinecones and acorns implied fertility.

At this festival of light, during Winter Solstice, we give deep thanks for the bringer of light, the sun, and all it contributes to our lives. We hang lights from our homes to illuminate the darkness and recall the rebirth of the light. Most cultures have celebrations during this time of the year, a time of the holy days and holidays.

Imbolc, a cross-quarter day, falls at the next turning of the Wheel and is celebrated on February 1st or 2nd. Also known as Brighid's day or Candlemas, it marks the starting point of spring. It is the time to call forth the idea seeds that have been germinating in the inner realm and that are now stirring with life, ready to grow during the upcoming cycle. A great opportunity exists during Imbolc to ceremonially create a "treasure map," a collage of pictures that represents what we want to manifest in our lives this year, as a visual reminder of the creations that are ready to sprout, grow and bear fruit.

Use Imbolc's energy of renewal for spring-cleaning of both home and body, to purify from the darker energy of winter. This point on the Wheel represents a potent time for creativity, invoking a muse, or starting a new project or initiation cycle.

Spring Equinox comes next as it bursts forth with the exuberance of the young, playful, and new. It falls sometime between March 21st to 23rd, during the time when light and dark exist in sacred balance. This time of year is named after the Earth Goddesses Ostara and Eostar. Since rabbits and eggs were sacred symbols of the fertile Goddesses, we see these used in many Spring Equinox celebrations.

We can use the window of Spring Equinox to add energy to our creations, to fill them with the life force this period offers. Connect to the enthusiasm of a youthful, lighthearted spirit by honoring children and the child within at this time as well. As one of the sacred points of balance during the year, Spring Equinox provides us with an opportunity to tune into the balance of our lives. Here we can evaluate things that may need our attention in order to come into greater harmony and alignment.

Beltane, or May Day, is celebrated on May 1st and is the starting point for the growing summer season. The young "sun" or "son" who was born at Winter Solstice has grown into a God and now becomes the partner of the Goddess in order to fertilize the fields for the abundant harvest. The Solar Fire God and the Earth Goddess unite now and bring forth life to feed the multitudes. This union of Earth and Fire is essential for the growth of crops, so it is honored with feasting and ceremony. Symbols and dances of sacred union and fertility abound at this time of year.

Each of us carries the two basic principles of masculine and feminine within our consciousness and at this time of year we find value in noticing how they are working together. Those two principles must join within for any creation to come to fruition. Honor how they both work, and notice what they want to fertilize with their combined energy. Bask in the beauty of this point of the seasonal cycle. Enjoy being outside, and give thanks to the marriage of Earth and Solar Fire, which bring us these gifts.

Summer Solstice, or midsummer, is the fullest point of the summer season. Occurring sometime around June 20th to 22nd, it is the longest day and shortest night of the year and serves as the subtle turning point when the light begins moving slowly back into darkness. During this time, we honor the abundance of the Earth Mother and the gift of warmth the sun brings forth. Here we work in ceremony with and celebrate fulfillment, passion, abundance, and manifestation.

Dancer Note:

The eight directions of the body - **croisé devant, à la quatriéme devant, écarté devant, à la seconde, épaulé derrière, à la quatrième derriere, croisé derriere, à la seconde other side** - are formed in the same wheel pattern that the Wheel of the Year is based on.

Musical Note:

Also, an eight-count phrase of music is done in the same rhythm as the wheel turns. **1**-2-3-4, **5**-6-7-8 with the strongest beats on the one and five just as the wheel changes from dark to light and light to dark on those same beats. Winter solstice (**1**)-2-3-4, Summer solstice (**5**)-6-7-8 it is a change in tempo at those same points.

Our creations will be starting to ripen if we have been energetically tending to them during the cycle. Tune into what else they may need now to come to fruition. Summer Solstice offers a perfect time to infuse them with the additional energy needed to complete their growth and to honor the growth they have made up to this point.

Lughnasad, also called Lammas, represents the first of three harvest festivals and is celebrated on August 1st or 2nd. Lammas means "loaf-mass," and this point on the Wheel honors the way sacred grain is transformed into bread: the seed of the grain is planted, then it grows, ripens, is harvested, and ground into flour. The flour itself goes through other layers of transformation as it is mixed with other ingredients to make dough, rises, is pounded down, and rises again before baking. Once the dough is baked and becomes bread, it is eaten and again transformed into fuel for the body.

During Lammas, we notice what is being harvested and transformed in our lives. Is there a place where we are releasing the grain from the chaff or pounding our creations down so they rise again in a fuller form? Lammas serves as a good time of year to pay attention to which part of the transformation cycle our creations may be in and, perhaps, to honor them in ceremony. Transformation, harvest, and gratitude all provide wonderful themes for working with this cross-quarter day, which starts the transition to fall.

Autumnal Equinox, also called Mabon, occurs somewhere around September 21st or 22nd. Sitting directly across the Wheel of the Year from Spring Equinox, here again we find light and dark perfectly balanced. As the halfway point from Summer Solstice to Winter Solstice, Autumnal Equinox brings with it the second harvest festival and the awareness that change is in the air. At this time of year, we let go of the growing cycle, allowing it to fall away just as the leaves fall from the trees.

As we honor and celebrate all that we have harvested in this growing cycle, we also notice what we need to leave behind. We ask ourselves, "What things in life do we need to release to a new home or to a new life?" Again, at this point in the Wheel cycle we are asked to look at where we need additional balance and to begin making the necessary changes. Also, we need to become aware of the preparations needed to support the inward journey we will take during the darker days ahead.

Finally, we move back again to the third harvest festival, Samhain, to complete the old year and begin a new one. Once more, this point moves us on to the rebirthing of the cycle, which corresponds to the point of its death.

The Earth's seasonal cycle can be likened to our daily cycle. One seasonal cycle to her is equivalent to one of our days. Spring represents her morning, summer her noon and afternoon, autumn her evening, and winter her night and deep sleep. She then wakes in the spring and begins her "day" all over again, just as we do.

The seasonal cycle also corresponds to the cycles we experience in the things we create, such as our lives, jobs, relationships, businesses, or projects. Everything we create goes through phases of development, in cycles that follow the same pattern we go through each day, each year, each lifetime. Their cycle has a beginning, morning, spring or child-like energy. Then, the cycle moves to a growing midday, summer, or adolescent energy. Next, the cycle evolves in maturity, to evening, autumn, or adulthood. From there it ends its cycle, in completion, night, winter, or elder years.

As we learn to understand and become aware of cycles, such as the

Wheel of the Year, we learn to handle life transitions much more effectively. If we can connect with the energy of those cycles and accept them as developmental phases through which we are passing, this helps us live in harmony with nature and life. If, on the other hand, we become comfortable with one phase or stage but not with another, we may try to cling to what we know, afraid to let go and to trust that the process will bring us to the next stage in just the right way and time. As we increase our comfort with all developmental phases, and the naturalness of change, through all parts of the cycle, we can accept the shifts that each phase brings rather than struggling against them as burdens or problems. Instead, we can honor what the new cycle gracefully brings as gifts and opportunities.

Each phase of the developmental cycle has its own kind of energy. During the phase of new beginnings, we experience the same abundant spring-like "growing energy" found in nature.

Wheel of the Year and the life cycle

Each point of the Wheel corresponds to a ten-year cycle of life.

Winter solstice	1	**Years 1-10**
Imbolc	2	**Years 10-20**
Spring Equinox	3	**Years 20-30**
Beltane	4	**Years 30-40**

50 is the gateway to the new pulse just like it is in music 1-2-3- 4 and the next measure 5-6-7-8. That is the reason 50 brings so many deep changes internally. it is literally entering a entirely new phrase or phase.

Summer Solstice	5	**Years 40-50**
Lammas	6	**Years 50-60**
Autumnal Equinox	7	**Years 60-70**
Samhain	8	**Years 70-80**

After eighty years a new cycle begins.

The new phase of something makes us energetic and enthusiastic, which helps us navigate a fairly large learning curve that usually accompanies this cycle. Just as there is so much to learn in childhood, this spring-like beginning phase finds us delving with eagerness and passion into the new and unexplored.

Moving into summer energy, we experience a sense of knowing and fullness. Just as in puberty, this phase contains a rich abundance of life-force energy. We channel the abundant life-force energy into our creations to invigorate the growth. In this phase we attend to our creation by watering, weeding, and applying the fertilizer of our attention.

When the fullness of our creation rises to its peak, and we harvest the fruit of our creation from what we have sown in our lives, we experience the energy of autumn. These equate to the years of adult maturity when we have reached our fullest potential and are reaping the rewards of our creations.

This phase moves us into winter. A more reflective time, winter often represents a time of transition to closure, the letting go phase before something ends and something new begins. This important phase of the cycle equates to our elder years when we may have less energy for the outer world and more energy for our inner work.

The developmental phases overlap one another within our lives. We can be in one phase in our life cycle, such as mid-adulthood but be in other phases in particular areas of our lives. For instance, we might be just starting a new business or job (spring/childhood), experiencing the fullness of our primary relationship (autumn/adulthood), and helping our elderly parents find comfort in closure (winter/elderhood). The more practice we gain at moving through transitions, the more comfortably we move to different phases. Our awareness and skill at moving through the transitions help to give us strength, courage, and comfort in times of great change, and increase our capacity for wholeness.

As she moves through her sacred dance of changing seasons, Earth helps us develop the capacity to embody wholeness. Through her cycles, she reminds us to have gratitude for our aliveness while honoring the vulnerability of death and closure. In her cycles, we learn that the Wheel of the Year, and the wheel of life encompass all aspects of living and dying. This balance of the cycles enacts the creational energy of the universal yin/yang principle. Possessing a true inner knowing of this principle helps us move through all parts of our lives with more trust in life itself. We appreciate the light and bright times that bring us into the outer world for growth, joy, and creativity, as well as those times that take us deep into the inner darkness for healing the soul, or for a journey with grief and loss.

By honoring the element of Earth, we create a container in our consciousness to hold the sacred in all life. When this developmental task is complete, we possess the knowing that indeed the earth and our bodies are sacred, as is all life in the material and physical realm -- our home, our finances, food, clothes, all the things that make up our world, lives, and physical creations.

At this point, we come to understand that even an act as simple as paying bills, cleaning house, or cooking a meal represents the sacred, and is as important as the holiest ritual. We now connect with the Divine in all aspects of lives. We see ourselves as sacred, holy, and whole just in being. We know that our essential nature is divine.

Connecting to Earth with an attitude of sacredness brings Spirit into our everyday lives and into all aspects of our lives. It deeply changes the energy of all that we create, aligning our creations with the greater good and with a higher purpose. Thus it brings the Divine into matter and form. When we work in this energy, all we do is in harmony with Spirit and carries the frequency of sacredness.

Exercise: Change

How comfortable are you with change? Do you find one aspect of the cycle of change easier than another? Take some time to journal about the cycle of change. You might start by thinking about letting go. Allow something to fall away, and something new to be seeded in your psyche. Incubate it in the dark, and birth it into the light of the outer world. Then tenderly nurture it in its young stages. Encourage its fullness. Harvest it. And then allow the old to fall away. What phase do you like the best? Which phase was harder for you? What does each aspect of the cycle want to share with you about its energy?

Additional Earth Mystery School Teachings

Abundance and Fertility

Mother Earth provides us with a wonderful example of the capacity to produce abundant supplies. By showing us her rich harvests and lush landscapes, she constantly teaches us about the availability of abundance and shows us that fertility abounds in every realm. Abundance often comes from a state of heart and mind alignment, through which we see the potential, the fullness available in each moment of life. Fertility can be found in ideas for new creations, sudden awarenesses or perceptions, and in our rich spiritual gifts.

Mother Earth also teaches us to create sustainable systems in all areas of life. We can learn to live in harmony with her and to replenish what we consume, thus ensuring that other people and other times will also experience abundance and fertility. When we take from the earth with no regard for the ways she naturally replenishes her system, we step out of balance with Earth's natural cycles, which can leave an area stripped and void of life. However, our ability to work in harmony with the earth keeps an area lush and helps it vibrantly renew its energy.

The same principle applies to our own life, bodies, and resources. When we work in harmony with the element of Earth, we learn to replenish abundance rather than simply use it. This harmonic way of personally enjoying tremendous abundance adds to the greater good of all, instead of taking away from others and the planet. When we can accomplish this, we let the old system of competition fall away and learn the language and systems of cooperation. We live in and create balance with the natural environment and with ourselves.

Beauty and Aesthetics

Beauty and aesthetics are primary teachings of Earth. Look around as you go out in nature, and notice the beauty of how the earth is formed. She is magnificent, especially in her natural, unaltered, and untouched state. Mother Earth's natural beauty uplifts our spirits and inspires us. Our own creations of beauty uplift and inspire us as well. When we go into a beautiful home, building, garden, or see a beautiful person, we are infused with inspiration. This kind of beauty is not based upon the current cultural definition of what we think of as beautiful or based on competitive or comparative references to other things of beauty. This beauty is found in all phases of development from youth to old age, in people of all races, and in all lands. Open to see the natural beauty of all beings and of all life.

Exercise: Creating Beauty

The more you allow yourself to create beauty in the world around you, the more you increase the vibration of your life. Choose something in your physical environment that you would consciously like to make more beautiful. It could be your body as you dress and adorn it. It could be a room or area of your home or office, or perhaps a place in your garden. Simply sit in the area or with your body and ask how it would like to express a greater level of beauty. Listen inside for the answer, and then create that new level of beauty. Once complete, notice how that feels and enjoy it.

Body Energy System

The body also speaks to us through the *chakras*,[3] one body energy system. Since these energetic languages are nonverbal, we have to practice decoding the information they give us. The physical body houses seven basic *chakras*, or energy systems. Each one is a unique system, and together they form a whole energy system of flow, balance, and integration. Each *chakra* corresponds to certain body parts and organs and to various facets of life.

The root *chakra* is located at the base of the spine, and corresponds to the legs, feet, and tailbone. Issues such as our survival, sense of security, and connection to our tribe live in this center. This *chakra* is positioned closest to the earth and is significant in our relationship to her. If we feel disconnected from the element of Earth or insecure in someway, pulling energy up from the earth can help to ground, anchor, and connect us to Earth's stable energy.

The second body center, the sacral *chakra,* is located in the lower abdomen just below the navel. This energy center provides the center for our sexuality, creativity, and abundance.

The third *chakra*, or solar plexus, is located in the upper abdomen, in the stomach area. The solar plexus serves as the seat of our personal power and of issues of self-esteem, responsibility, and self-respect.

The fourth *chakra*, the heart center, is located in the center of the chest. Here we experience love, grief, compassion, and kindness.

The fifth body center, or throat *chakra,* is located in the throat area. Here we work with our personal will and the expression of truth.

The sixth energy center, or brow *chakra,* is located in the forehead. Here we think, evaluate, and learn from our experiences in concrete, abstract, and intuitive ways.

The crown *chakra*, or seventh energy center, is located at the top of the head. Here our relationship to Spirit connects us with the spiritual realm.

The body energy system is an important part of the study of the element of Earth. Attune to each chakra. Knowing that the body's energy centers are a subtle aspect of our physical form, feel the unique energies of each center. Feel how your body holds energy differently in each center, and how it contains the various aspects of your life experience. Practice sensing the way your body has stored your unique life experiences in these distinct centers. The more you clear your chakra and energy system, releasing any dense energy or energetic blocks, the more room you make in your body for your desires to come into form. As the debris from old experiences is released, the space for new creation comes into existence. (If you want more information on the chakras, many wonderful books have been written on the subject to take you further in your development and understanding.)

Body Wisdom

The body speaks to us with subtle messages, sending signals when it needs movement, is thirsty, hungry, ready for rest, and so on. If we are listening, the body's wisdom offers us the guidance we need for good health, nutrition, and exercise. In addition to subtly guiding us to what it needs for its well-being, the body also brings us messages for living our lives. By increasing our capacity to listen to the ways our body talks to us, we can hear these messages. Often they do not come in words; they are spoken in delicate and refined feelings of openness, constriction, discomfort, and, if we are still not listening, possibly pain. Our body will clearly tell us its wisdom if we will listen, and when we learn to listen well, we increase our health and well being tremendously.

When we work with a personal issue or concept, whether it is emotional, mental, active, or spiritual, it is extremely important that we include the body in the process. The body offer us information about that issue or concept, thus helping us move through or understand it. If we want to clear old thoughts or energetic blocks around something, we must do that on all levels -- emotional, intellectual, energetic, spiritual, and physical. Plus, to fully use any new knowledge, skill, or belief system, it is essential to embody the concepts, to literally take the knowing into the body by physically activating the learning in a way that is appropriate for the subject. Open to further acknowledge body wisdom as an important tool -- not only for health, but also for life guidance -- and see what gifts it brings.

Exercise: Receiving Body Guidance

There is a wonderful way to get a simple "yes" or "no" answer when you ask the body a question. Place your awareness in your heart center and say to yourself, "yes." Notice how the "yes" feels in your body. For some it feels full, expansive, and free. Now say, "no" and see how that feels in your body. For some it feels closed, tight, and constricted. Your body's response to the words may feel different than this, and that is fine. Simply notice how the words feel to you. Now say "yes" again and then "no," and feel the shift in energy and emotion. If you have a question about your life, ask your body and feel its guidance. Is it answering "yes" or "no"? Also, just before you are about to do something, try simply noticing which sensations you feel. Does your body feel open and expansive or tight and closed? Your body is talking to you, telling you if it wants to take that action or not. By taking the time to listen to your body, you learn when you are out of alignment with this physical part of yourself. Including your body in your decisions will help you proceed in a more balanced and harmonious manner.[4]

Ceremony & Celebration

Ceremony provides a way to honor our physical world transitions and bridges our inner world with the outer world. Ceremony gives us a powerful, safe, and sacred container in which to commemorate life changes, such as the changing of the seasons, the birth of a child, a marriage, the passage into adulthood or into elderhood. It can mark the transition of death or divorce, a move to a new home, or the start of a new job. If appropriate to the occasion, celebration can raise the energy of a ceremony to a joyful level. For more on ceremony see the Elemental Tools chapter.

Containment

A foundational expression of the element of Earth, containment refers to the ability to create vessels, containers, and physical boundaries. Earth uses its containment ability to create our individual homes and our bodies. The Earth of our bodies holds and contains our feelings, our life force, our intellect, and our spirit. Without the density of Earth and the ability to move Earth substance into form, we would be unable to have an experience of the physical world. The element of Earth contains our human experience.

Earth as a planet also creates the larger container of our physical experience. Earthly containment works in conjunction with all the other elements. We need containers to hold water so we can get it from place to place, candle holders and fireplaces to keep our home flames contained, lungs to hold the air necessary to animate our physical form, and a body to hold the spirit that allows us to express in this realm.

When working with Earth to create an idea in the physical realm or to create greater levels of wholeness, we often need a greater level of containment to achieve our goal. A space, or a larger space, needs to be created internally or externally for the idea or thing to take shape and develop within. An example of an internal container might be the time and space free from distraction in which an author can write a book. Space and time create the container. An example of a physical container can be as simple as a pot chosen in which to plant flowers or the walls that create a room.

We create a larger internal container for wholeness each time we integrate concepts that seem opposed to one another. As we develop our ability to hold something as "both/and" instead of just "either/or," our capacity for wholeness increases and our ability to hold and work effectively with larger and larger systems expands. For example, once we have contained and integrated the Wheel of the Year within ourselves, we can add -- make room for -- another level of knowledge into that system, such as the integration of moon cycles or astrology. Once we can achieve containment effectively, either externally or internally, we can increase our capacity to handle new systems, developmental stages, knowledge, and experiences by adding additional containers to hold these things.

Earth-Based Spirituality

The basis for any earth-based spirituality lies in honoring and connecting to nature. Many earth-based paths to spirituality exist, some more formal than others. Each path and indigenous culture has its own ways of connecting to the Great Spirit and Mother Earth.

Some people only need nature as their temple and connection point to the Divine, while others prefer the more formalized setting and structure of organized religion. Still others prefer both, a nature based spirituality and a formalized religious structure. Each of us must find the path that resonates with our own inner wisdom.

Foundations

Earth teaches us to build good strong foundations for our lives and for our projects. Since Earth is literally the ground upon which we stand, it teaches us to create solid support for anything we build. Through Earth we learn to stand our ground and to stand on our own. We learn to take and complete one step at a time until our physical-realm projects are completed. Earth helps us understand that we are able to move to the next juncture only when all aspects of the previous phase are finished and not before. The way to expand and grow in the earthly realm lies in ensuring that all aspects of our life foundation are handled effectively; then we can expand to the next level or levels.

Earth teaches us to take responsibility for the foundational structures in all areas of our life. A house, for example, needs the foundation laid before the rest of the structure can be built. Likewise, we need the foundation of our lives to function smoothly before we can expand our life structure by creating anew. We require that our physical needs be met before we can do much else; we need to know if we will have something to eat and to wear, if we will have a warm and dry place to sleep. Having those aspects of our lives in order gives us the capacity to go to the next level -- going to work, paying our bills, being in relationship, exercising, and enjoying ourselves. When our foundation is in chaos -- when our basic needs are unmet, it makes it extremely difficult to bring new things into structure and form. Order represents an important facet of structure and form. To create a more evolved structure, we need our current foundation to be strong and orderly.

Exercise: Foundation Review

Is your foundation in place for you to stand solidly on your own? Do you maintain your foundation and the matter of your life easily or do you struggle with keeping your things in order? Is your home in order? Your car? Your finances? Your closet? Your yard? Your body? Your business? How about all those ideas you are creating and bringing into form -- are they complete? Or do you have tons of ideas started but not completed? Are you consciously maintaining what you currently own? Do you surround yourself with beauty? Are you filled with gratitude for all that is in your life at this moment? Ask the element of Earth to work with you if you need help in these areas.

Gratitude

The soul quality of gratitude is developed with a deep trust and respect for Earth. When we feel grateful for all that we have been given and treat those gifts with respect, our lives reflect that energy. Gratitude creates an internal quality of grace that allows us to bring our own creativity into form and to anchor it fully on Earth. When we approach life with an attitude of appreciation and fill all that we do and have with the frequency of gratitude, we attract matter of a higher frequency into our lives in greater abundance. In addition, energy lines up to help us fulfill our desires. Make it a practice to express gratitude daily.

Exercise: Gratitude

Make some time for yourself to connect with the soul quality of gratitude. In your elemental journal, make a list of all the things for which you are grateful in your life. Notice how you feel after you have completed the list. Do you consciously and continuously recognize the gifts you have in life? Do you honor the realm of Earth and express your gratitude for it?

Grounded

Earth teaches us to become grounded in our lives and actions, to solidly take care of our lives and our bodies. When we have lots of ideas but rarely bring them fully into form, becoming more grounded or down-to-earth may help us do so. We may need to balance our Air, Water, or Fire with greater amounts of Earth. If more grounding is needed, we can go outside and stand on the earth. Then we can send our energy down or draw up Earth energy through our legs and ask Earth to ground our actions and our beings in the physical world. Likewise, we can ask Earth in what areas we need to become more grounded, and listen for her reply internally. Be mindful to thank her for her assistance.

Honoring Cycles

Earth and her changing seasons teach us of transitions, change, and how to honor the cycles of life. She teaches us about allowing the old to fall away and the new to be seeded and grow in darkness until a new shoot develops. She shows us how to tend to what is growing and developing so we may reap the rewards of a bountiful harvest. When we learn to connect with the Earth cycle, we learn to handle our own life transitions more effectively. We begin living in harmony with life, increasing our comfort with all phases so we can gracefully accept the gifts that each new cycle brings.

Nature

Spending time in the natural world uplifts us and brings us back into soul alignment, because being in nature links us back to our own basic nature. The natural world connects directly through the elemental forces to the source of divine energy. So, when we spend time in nature, we connect to the life-force energy of the organic physical world, and that energizes and restores our personal life-force. Nature balances the energy systems of the body by aligning and harmonizing us with the living field of creation.

The more deeply we immerse ourselves in a natural setting or the more time we spend outside, the more uplifting and re-energized we can become. We can even consciously engage the elemental forces to assist us when we are in nature. For example, when we inhale, we can ask that the life force from nature come in through our breath and then release what we no longer need as we exhale. This process happens to some degree just by being outside, but when we ask consciously for this process to occur, our life-force increases tremendously. When we go into nature at a power time, such as at a Wheel of the Year point or a new or full moon, or when we go to a powerful sacred site, we receive an additional boost of energy from the natural world.

Organic Timing

Nature has its own kind of timing. It responds to an inner sense when things are ripe and ready to pick or to deliver. We can't keep nature on a time clock or a calendar for precise predictability. To understand this, consider a tomato, which is ready for picking only when it is ripe. We can't schedule according to the calendar exactly what day that tomato will need to be picked. We can have some idea how long it takes to ripen based on our past experience with tomatoes, but we cannot know with certainty what day and time any of the fruit will be ready. It helps to remember that while our calendars were derived by witnessing nature's timing, she does not necessarily abide by those structures herself. Her time is her own. Often we need to regain our own sense of organic timing, allowing things in our lives to ripen on their own schedule, and picking the fruit only when it is truly ready to be harvested.

Priestess/Priest Within

The internal archetypes of Priestess and Priest hold the container for the expression of the sacred on earth and perform a vital function in human consciousness.[5] Working with the Priest/ess archetype, we learn to become the empty vessel, the chalice, or the hollow bone, which enables us to bring forth divine energies and anchor them onto the earth plane. We learn to stay in a place of receptivity, receiving the information and subtle vibrations of Divinity. This state of receptivity is the place of not knowing. With the help of our inner Priest/ess, we learn to release the ego's need "to know" or "to have the answer" and acquire the ability to hold an empty container so the pure awareness of the Divine can fill it.

As we activate the Priest/ess archetype within, we access our own connection to the Divine directly. This releases our need for an outer world intermediary such as a Priest, Minister, Shaman or Guru to connect to Spirit for us. While we may appreciate and learn from another's teachings, insights, and connection to Spirit, we also have the ability to create our own direct connection to the Divine.

The Priest/ess represents the aspect of self that sees all life and all life experience -- from worship, to preparing a meal, to bill paying -- as sacred. It knows that simply being in physical form is sacred. Forming and working with Earth with a sacred attitude brings Spirit into our everyday life. It brings the Divine into matter and form.

Stewardship

We are the stewards of all the physical matter in our lives: our bodies, homes, finances, land, and businesses. We have the responsibility to mindfully and respectfully nurture and manage the matter in our lives. We need to be able to release all that no longer vibrationally matches our lives, letting go of old clothes, books, photographs, home accessories, etc., when we no longer need them. This process creates energetic and physical space for the new to come in.

Tending

We move in right relationship to the material world as we learn to honor the physical realm of matter. Earthly things need tending: our bodies, homes, cars, gardens, clothes, and finances. All things of Earth need to be cared for. They require upkeep, cleaning, refreshment, and maintenance. We must fully honor matter and the physical realm and tend to our earthly realm.

Consider finances, for instance. They require on-going care and tending. We need to make sure our supply of money exceeds our demand. In other words, we must ensure that we have a sufficient amount of money coming in to cover our expenses. We need to monitor our finances regularly so we notice any changes in our spending or expenses and adjust accordingly. We learn to do this with the structure of a budget and by tending to that structure on a regular basis. The same holds true for our investments, insurance policies, and all other components of our financial lives. We can apply this tending principle to most areas of our physical lives.

Touch

Touch symbolizes the ecstatic gift of the physical realm. In our body, we are able to experience the ecstasy of an embrace, the joy of a child's hand held in our own, the fulfillment of food on our tongue, the chill of ice on our skin, the solidity of the ground under our feet as we walk, skip, and dance. Earth is an amazingly rich planet, and with our body's ability to touch, we have the vehicle to experience it.

Sweet Earth, we thank you for the gift of this physical realm in which we live. Please receive our gratitude for your teachings, your wisdom, your beauty, your containment, and your rich abundant blessings.
Thanks be.

CHAPTER FOUR

Water

"To watch us dance is to hear our hearts speak."

Hopi Indian Saying

Water

Emotional Realm

Mystery School Teachings:
Inner child work, self-esteem, mirror of relationships, development of emotional maturity.

Developmental Task:
Running clear, clean, current emotional water

Key Word: Clear

Soul Quality: Love

Ecstatic Realm: Play

Primary Power: Using Love as a force

Level 2 Power: Infusion

Natural Rhythm Cycle: Moon Phases

Water's potent ways of teaching are as varied as the forms she takes -- oceans, rivers, lakes, streams, rain, drinking water, ice, hot water, bathing water, hail, snow, sleet. With just as many variations, internally Water teaches us through the realm of feelings and emotions. We experience feelings that run cold, frozen, steamy, hot, smooth, gentle, calm, or like a rough day out at sea.

Our emotions provide important guidance and teachings about our lives, and each of us possesses a different comfort level when it comes to feeling and working with them. Few of us were taught how to honor and work with our emotions as children, and yet emotional maturity is an essential component for full effectiveness in the world. Water teaches us to find greater levels of emotional safety in our relationships and to express more of who we are in the world.

We learn to develop our emotional awareness through Water's ability to mirror ourselves back to us.[1] Water is the only element in which we can see our own reflection. If we learn to hear Water's message, we will find that how we experience everything in our lives reflects our own inner world -- how we see and feel about our lives. If we look at our reflection, we are shown what we believe about the world and ourselves. Water teaches us through our reflections to develop emotionally and to gain emotional maturity.

Water coaches us to greater self-awareness through our relationship to our inner child, our relationship to ourselves, and our relationship with others. Water shows us how to run a clear, clean, emotional current, to learn to respond to life instead of react to it, to activate the power of love, to access the ecstatic level through play, and to wash away old wounds so we can create space for a new vibration to be held by the water in our bodies.

In addition to teaching us, the essence of Water can nourish, clear, heal, and inspire us. Our primal connection with Water begins in the womb, which may be why we feel soothed and nurtured by being in or close to Water. Walking by the ocean, floating in a lake, sitting next to a beautiful stream, or even climbing into a tub of warm water can bring upon us deep feelings of quiet nurturance. Water quenches our thirst, nourishes us body and soul, and teaches us how to dance to the natural rhythm of our hearts.

Water Skills and Powers

A highly programmable element, Water merges with and holds the vibration of any message it is given. The energy that is infused into Water becomes the emotional tone it holds. Our bodies contain a large percentage of Water and our inner Water contains both our consciously chosen and our unconscious thoughts and feelings. Our inner Water creates our emotional tone, which others around us can feel just by being connected to us.

When we come into contact with others, our feeling energy merges with their feeling energy almost like drops of water merging together to form a stream. If we are at all aware when we walk into a room, for instance, we can sense if someone is upset or happy, because their mood permeates the emotional climate of that environment. The good news is we have the capacity to alter the tone Water holds, even the Water in our bodies, and we can uplift or shift an emotional climate.

Our thoughts and prayers affect the watery emotional tone of our own inner world, as well as of the world of something or someone to which we are connected. What we infuse into the water of any emotional climate including ourselves, affects the whole. If we add love and upliftment, such as in the form of positive thoughts, blessings, or prayers our intent assists the situation and softens the emotional energy.

To increase our consciousness with Water, we need to become aware of how our emotional state affects a situation and how our thoughts permeate our inner Water. Even in the face of fear, we can infuse the situation with the energy we want it to hold by choosing to hold the vibrational tone of love. Learning to increase our capacity with Water requires that we take greater and greater levels of personal responsibility for the infusion of our thoughts, prayers, and feelings into the emotional container of any situation.

Example of Love and Fear

On a mid-summer day in 2002, while preparing for a talk on the elements I was giving the next day, I decided to go out in nature to go deeper into my own inner nature. I went to a beautiful mountain state park in Northern Georgia called Raven Cliff. I stopped at the first campsite along the stream, which is just a short walk from the parking area. I spread out my blanket, made myself comfortable, then prepared to begin one of my favorite meditations. First, I connected to Earth, my body, and the ability to bring things into structure and form in the physical realm, and I gave thanks to the spirit of the place, the trees, and the land around me. Then, I connected to Water, the creek I was next to, my feelings, and the deep nourishment that comes from water. Next, I connected to Air and uplifted my thoughts and energy. I felt the sun on my face and connected to Fire and the life-force that flows through all things. I thanked Spirit for the opportunity to be there, and then I began my meditation.

The spot where I was sitting wasn't far off the path, and in the fifteen minutes I was sitting there ten to twelve people passed talking loudly. I kept wondering if a quieter spot would have been a better choice, but I decided to stay where I was.

When I was complete, I walked to the water and stood facing down stream to ask Water to assist me in releasing old energy that needed to leave – especially old fears, feelings, and beliefs. Then I asked for something unusual. I asked Water to release from me anything that it felt needed to go that I hadn't considered. I then turned upstream to bring in the new and consciously opened myself to receive abundance, grace, and love. As I was thinking about what else to open to, I looked across the stream and saw a black bear standing about eight to ten feet away on the shore ledge on the other side. A cub stood on the embankment behind her and a splash a little bit further downstream drew my attention to a second cub in the water.

At once I moved into an altered state of awareness activated by a sudden adrenalin flood of fear rushing through my body. In the slow, dreamlike state of awareness in which I found myself, I believed the bear would just walk away on her side of the stream and all would be fine. Instead, as I slowly began backing up, she started coming toward me. I called silently for protection and tried to remember what I'd heard about how to behave around bears. All I could remember was not to run. As she came across the stream, I noticed she actually had three good size cubs with her. I tried to stay calm and to slowly move out of her path, but she kept coming toward me.

Since I could think of nothing else to do, I decided to concentrate on opening my heart to send her love. I hid behind a tree, centered myself, and poured love not just to the bear and her cubs but into the whole area. She kept coming toward me, so I again backed up, while realizing there was no good way for me to maneuver out of the area without turning my back on the bears. I moved behind a larger tree and again poured love out of my heart toward her and the cubs. The bear kept moving in an effort to see me, and I kept moving around the tree attempting to stay out of her line of sight. At one point, I knew she was close to the tree and I wanted to know where she was, so I peered around the left side of the tree only to find all three cubs were looking straight at me. I was entranced by how cute they were, but had to actively continue sending them love as I simultaneously experienced the most intense fear I had ever felt. I then internally said, "Spirit, the one thing I need this bear to do is to please leave the area." To my surprise, the bear then turned and walked off away from me, her cubs following behind her.

Next to witnessing my nephew's first breath and my sister's last breath, my encounter with the bear and her cubs afforded me the most amazing experience of the power of life and nature I have had to date. Looking that mama bear in the eye took me right to the fear of death. She could have decided I would make a good lunch, but fortunately she didn't. I am grateful that, in the time she was there, I was able to call on my ability to love -- not just to fear -- and that she graced me so deeply with her presence.

Thanks to my work with the elements, I understood from Air how much my intention "of being protected" would assist me in the situation. I knew how much my vibration affects the world around me, and I realized that sending the bears the vibration of love was the only power I possessed in that moment that could assist me. In addition, Water actively has taught me to choose love in the face of fear, and I was able to do just that during a time of enormous testing. Fire has been teaching me for years just how much personal power I have the ability to access. As four-legged animals that represent Earth, the bears gave me a direct experience of what happens to the world around me when I rise above my fear and walk in a space of love.

Holding that much fear and that much love at the same time shifted something deep within me. I now truly know that each of us can choose to hold and send love in the face of fear. So many people think it is necessary to get rid of fear first before they can focus on love, but, in truth, you can feel the most fear you've ever felt and still choose to send love at the same time.

Throughout our lives, Water develops our emotional capacity. We start learning about emotions from the emotional climate of our family, caretakers, and those we grow up around. The emotional maturity of our caretakers determines the emotional maturity with which we initially feel comfortable. Our family and those with whom we grew up initially help to define the way we treat ourselves and others emotionally, and often determine the amount of love we are comfortable giving and receiving.

Until we are aware and capable enough to change our Water tone or energy, we absorb the emotional climate around us, which explains why those with whom we spend our early years so affect our emotional lives later on. We have absorbed their emotional energy and made it our own. In fact, we start absorbing the emotional tone around us from the time of our conception. Water served as the medium of our conception: the sperm traveled on the lubrication of fertile watery fluid to the egg, and then, as a fetus, we grew in the deep amniotic fluid of the womb. Even as we were developing in the womb, we also began absorbing the emotional vibrations of our family's dynamics.

If as babies or young children we were wanted, not wanted, loved, pushed away, held, yelled at, spanked, abused, or supported, all these ways in which we were treated and thought about were soaked up into our emotional bodies and then spilled out into our cellular structure. Those who raised us created an emotional aquarium in which we now swim -- at least until we consciously create a new emotional container of our own. Our caretakers may have had an unconscious aquarium of their own, built by someone else and in which all their old emotional programs still ran. Or they may have been conscious enough to have cleared their emotional vibration, thus making the aquarium they built for us less "dirty" and in

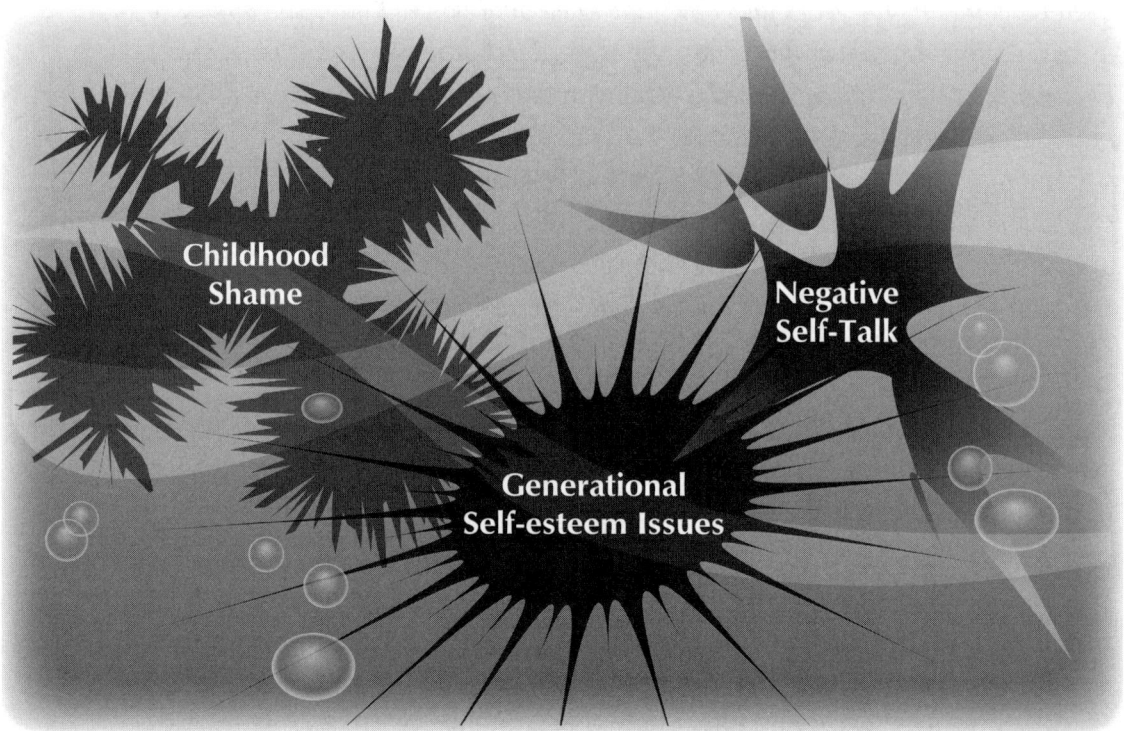

need of cleaning and redesign. Either way, they did the best they could at that time in their lives to influence our emotional education.

Families as a whole tend to hold in their unconscious emotional waters all kinds of beliefs about how life and others will treat them. These include beliefs that begin with phrases such as "men will...,women will...,the government does.., children are..., money is..., doctors will..., religion is..., nature is." They also include statements about what we can or cannot do and what capacity we have to affect our world. Every belief we hold about the world programs our emotional waters in some way and all our beliefs, including those about our worth and value in life, are held in the watery cells of our bodies. These old emotional "programs" can "junk up" our systems until we clear them out. Once old energies are cleared, we gain the ability to infuse our clear clean Water realm with what we choose for it to hold and the energy with which we want it to vibrate.

If we want to grow beyond our current emotional dynamics, we need to become more conscious and aware of what we feel at any given moment. We can start increasing our emotional awareness by noticing what part of our consciousness is responding or reacting to life. If our child consciousness or ego state[2] (the inner child mentioned previously) is reacting, for example, we may demand that our needs get met right now by those around us. We may feel small and weak or guilty. We may be unwilling to take responsibility for the situation in which we find ourselves and become withdrawn, detached, distant, or overly insistent about our needs.

If the part of us that contains our adolescent energy reacts we may sound sarcastic and feel rebellious. From this level of consciousness we frequently act in ways that do not support our larger life vision. We may refuse to be told what to do. Sometimes we may clearly say we won't fulfill a request, or we may just passively avoid doing it. We may be unwilling to express how we truly feel about a situation and think others have control over our life.[3]

We sometimes approach life from our inner parent. This part of us can sound as though we know what is best for others, more than they know for themselves. From this ego place, we can be inflexible, hypercritical, disapproving, righteous, and judgmental with ourselves and with others. When functioning from our inner parent we also can try to defend, shield, and rescue those around us, thus becoming the overly responsible hero parent.[4]

From our adult state, we are able to consider our options and respond effectively to a situations. We are connected to our own sources of wisdom -- our feelings, inner guidance, and intuition. We are able to take healthy responsibility, rather than too much or too little. Instead of acting out of unconscious emotional states from the past, we make choices about situations from the present moment.[5]

When we are in an unconscious emotional ego state, we may draw someone to us to play another role. For instance, if we are acting from our child or adolescent state, we may draw a parent type to us to be disapproving and vice versa. Only two people in their adult states can interact in a conscious manner as equals.

As we begin to develop our capacity to know our emotional state, we can expand our ability to respond from an adult inner state to the situations in our lives. We become capable of responding to life from this emotionally mature place, and do so regardless of the emotional state in which others around us may show up. It takes time, awareness, patience, and self-love to develop into an emotionally mature person. We need to learn to listen to our feelings as guidance too, and to know that our feelings are powerful and important teachers.

The soul essence of love exists in the element of Water. The clearer our emotions, the more space there is for love to move in our life. In the emotional realm we learn to love ourselves fully, to nurture, to heal the inner child, and to create a space for clarity, flow, and love to move freely in our relationships with others. Water serves as our teacher of how to become emotionally mature, how to care for ourselves emotionally, and how to "respond" instead of "react" to life and others.

At the center of the emotional realm lies the heart, the seat of unconditional love and the place where relationship to self and others is deeply nurtured and held. Manifesting unconditional love often requires us to realize that all that happens in life represents part of the process of our development. We learn through Water to let go of how we think things are supposed to be and to love people even when their path takes them in a different direction than ours. Most importantly, we learn to love ourselves despite the things that may look to us like mistakes.

Our life path with Water revolves around the development of emotional maturity. Emotional maturity means knowing the difference between a reaction and a response. An emotional reaction is when we reply to a situation from an unconscious emotional state before we give ourselves time to choose our response. A reaction can take the form of speaking harshly or of an extreme act of physical violence. It takes emotional work to learn to listen to and deal constructively with our emotions, to learn to relate to ourselves and to others non-judgmentally, and to respond to situations instead of reacting to them. As we learn to relate to ourselves and to others from a space clear of judgment and to respond rather than react to situations, we deepen our development of emotional maturity. Open-hearted and free-flowing, we learn the gifts of Water and its emotional realm.

As we clear and clean our emotional current, a force increases its flow through us, Water's primary power of love. The more space we create for love to run in our emotional waters, the more it infuses our bodies and our lives, adding a quality of grace to all that it touches. This type of love is a force, not just romantic love. Love used as a powerful force infuses everything with which it comes into contact, and provides the nourishment needed for things to grow and flourish.

Without Water or love, things in our lives wither and die. Yet love applied to our relationships, children, and businesses -- and even to ourselves -- deeply nourishes them and provides the elemental juice they need for growth. As we turn our attention to each thing in our lives, we want to notice which ones need more of the Water power of love. Is there anything to which we have neglected applying this healing balm? Just as in the heat of the summer our flowers need water daily, the substance of our lives often needs the application of this element. Start applying love to all you touch and notice the deep shift as its power is applied.

Activation: Water's Primary Power of Love

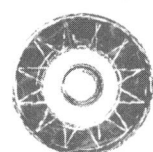

Preferably, do this exercise standing. If for any reason you cannot stand up to do it, your intention will work to activate the power even while seated. Find a great piece of music that feels watery or loving to you. Before putting on the music, state either out loud or silently in your head your intention to activate Water's power of love. Place your awareness in your body, then put on your music and dance to activate, enliven, and embody your intention. Once complete with the dance, put your awareness in your heart area, and ask what else you need to know about using the Water power of love in your life. Then listen for the answer and journal about the response you receive.

Exercise: Water Ceremony to Increase Self-Love

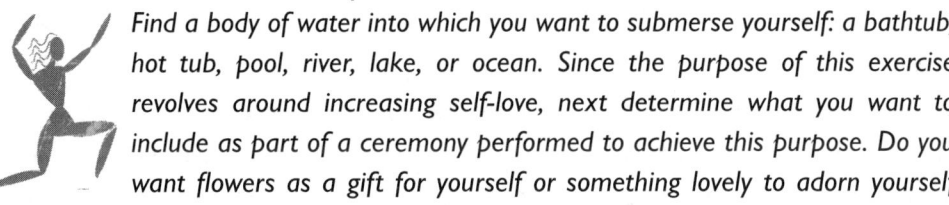

Find a body of water into which you want to submerse yourself: a bathtub, hot tub, pool, river, lake, or ocean. Since the purpose of this exercise revolves around increasing self-love, next determine what you want to include as part of a ceremony performed to achieve this purpose. Do you want flowers as a gift for yourself or something lovely to adorn yourself with when you are complete? Do you want candlelight or beautiful music? What else are your soul and spirit calling for you to include in the ceremony? Before you enter the body of water, give thanks for all Water does to support life in our world and in your body. Truly and deeply express your gratitude. You may want to call in sacred space or express gratitude for the other elements, inner guides, people in your life, or whatever you feel moved to speak about. When you are steeped in gratitude, ask the water to cleanse, relax, and release any places within you that need to be freed to make room for more self-love in your body. Once you feel clear and clean, open to receive and infuse yourself with deep self-love. As you complete the ceremony, notice the difference in how you feel, and give thanks once again.

Water cleans the physical realm. Air blows things off and dries or shifts something energetically. Fire will reduce something to ashes. More Earth just makes things dirtier. The earthly realm needs cleaning, and Water is the element that accomplishes that. We wash our clothes, our dishes, our physical bodies, our homes, and our cars -- most all the material and physical things that make up our lives -- with water.

The same holds true in our emotional realm. Emotional water needs to be kept clear, clean, and flowing with the current. Interestingly, the only way to clear the emotional body and move emotions is by actually feeling them. We can't use Air and think about them; that simply blows emotions around and adds to our confusion. We can't apply Fire and distract ourselves with action or bury them in Earth, our body, without finding ourselves later dealing with an issue caused by them surfacing in some way. To clean out emotions, we actually have to feel them.

We cannot block ourselves from feeling emotions and move the emotions at the same time. Just as the flow of water needs to be released for a river to run smoothly, so must our feelings move and flow freely by being felt. Learning to fully feel our emotions requires skill, one important to open to if we are to use Water in alignment with the other elements in our co-creations.

We can move our feelings in many healthy ways, such as through expressive art, dance, role-playing, journaling, with the kind ear of a good friend or therapist, or simply by allowing ourselves to feel our emotions without reacting to them. The more we take the time to respond to our deep feelings, the clearer, cleaner, and more current our emotional Water becomes, which enhances our ability to infuse our inner Water for co-creation.

Water's secondary power is found in its capacity to be infused with the energy we choose for it to carry. Once we have completed the secondary power of Earth and are in full alignment with heaven and earth, we possess a tremendous capacity to run energy through our bodies to infuse Water. Blessed or holy water has been touted for centuries for a variety of uses. Water that has been blessed has vast healing power, and people flock to sacred waters to receive gifts and blessings. Many parts of the world stake claim to sacred waters and we use this holy water for many types of ceremonies, from baptisms to healing the sick.

The priests and priestesses in Peru used to charge the local water with healing energy for the entire area before it was sent to water the crops.[6] We can charge our own water for ceremony by infusing it with blessings and prayers before we use it. There are also things we can do to uplift the water on the planet, such as consciously thanking it for the work it does to nourish us and sending our prayers into it.

We can be mindful of emptying plastic bottles before discarding or recycling them so the water isn't trapped in the bottle for as long as it takes plastic to break down. Additionally, consider the water it takes to produce the plastic bottles themselves and how long it takes them to break down. The more we can utilize water filters the more we honor the aliveness of Water. We also can increase our mindfulness about the products we clean with and use on our gardens. Is the product environmentally friendly or harmful to our precious water supply? Try to use only those that are friendly.

Our prayers and mindfulness can help keep the water on the planet clean and vibrant for the generations to come. With the actions we take towards water and the energy and love with which we infuse it, we can choose to be part of the solution of clear, clean water for the planet. Water does so much for us. Let us remember to be thankful and loving to it often.

Activation: Level Two Power - Infusing Water

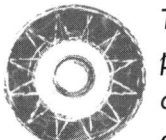
This activation becomes even more powerful once all the elemental primary powers have been activated. You will need a container of water for this activation. Start by aligning your body with Earth and sky, and then ask the energy of the Divine to run through you and into your hands. Simply place your hands over or around the container of water and call forth the energy you want for infusion, and send the energy into the water. It is important that the energy be of a loving, thankful, prayer-filled vibration.

Exercise: Creating with Water

You can do quite a variety of things to activate the Water teachings for yourself. For this exercise, try using your creativity and the element of Water by allowing your feelings to surface, and then creating a watercolor picture to represent that feeling. After you finish, notice the difference between your Earth exercise working with clay and Water's exercise of painting with watercolors. How does water feel as a medium in your creations? You may also want to try activating your connection to Water by doing a water dance and feeling the energy of flow in your body.

Water's Developmental Task

Our drinking water is best when clear, clean, and flowing freely, and the same for our emotional state. If our emotions become backed up, old, and stagnant, we lose the sense of aliveness and freshness that clear, clean, and current emotional Water brings. We can start working with this concept simply by noticing how we feel. In other words, we just tune into our feelings and ask, "How am I feeling?" An important next step involves noticing when we have feelings of discomfort of any type. As we learn the language of emotions, we begin to tune into our feelings and to name them. We learn to become comfortable discussing our feelings. If we don't recognize some feelings, we can describe what sensations they bring up in our bodies. If tears fill our eyes, it is important to find a way or place to let them flow, they represent an energy in motion and need to move. Tears are deeply clearing and cleansing.

Once we are more practiced, we can begin noticing and tuning into how we feel on a consistent basis. At that point, we will begin to notice quickly when a feeling needs to be addressed at a deeper level. Let's say we tune into our feelings and notice that when someone makes a particular comment we have a tendency to react with anger. Noticing this feeling response allows us to go deeper into our understanding of the reaction and to discover what triggered the reaction. Did it touch on an old wound? Does it bring up an old feeling of lack of self-worth? Does it remind us of feelings we had as a child? Do we sense we are being insulted and feel the need to address the issue? We need to notice and tune into where the feeling takes us internally.

Let's call those places inside where we have a reaction "charges"[7] -- a place where the energy of something gets larger than life, gets filled with extra juice. Charges provide great feeling guides to what we need to clear up to keep our emotional realm running cleanly and clearly.

Charges are like trash in the water that we need to notice and clear away. Clearing a charged issue may take some time initially, but as we learn to do this, our life will become smoother and more fluid. We want the water realm to be like a beautiful mountain stream flowing clear, and clean. One way to keep our emotional realm unobstructed involves discussing with those around us the truth of how we feel in a blame-free manner. When we blame others, they may end up feeling defensive, and we may end up in a fight over who is right and who is wrong. From that position nothing gets resolved -- especially not our emotions. We need to learn to hold a space for others to hear us and to be heard without the conversation being about right and wrong. So often people have grown up in

Dancer Note:
The moon also moves to the same **4/4** time as the wheel of the year.
The beat of the phrases happens at the new and full moon.

an environment where issues and feelings have to be someone's fault. If we truly want to be heard and to clear up an emotional issue with someone, we want to create a safe space in which to speak our truth and in which others can speak theirs.

Let's look at the difference between a charged and an uncharged situation. Imagine a scene where someone just told you to take out the garbage. A defensive reaction might go something like this: "Don't tell me when to take out the garbage. I'll do it when I feel like it." Do you feel the "charge" in that type of reaction?

An uncharged response might sound like this: "You know, when you tell me to take out the garbage, I remember being scolded as a child and I find myself getting angry at being told when to do something. I wonder what that is about for me?" The person hearing the second version is going to have a much different response to what you are saying than the first version. The conversation that follows is likely to be much healthier and to allow everyone to stay feeling connected to each other.

Most of us were not trained in relationship skills at home or at school. We became accustomed to less than clear, clean communication between people, and, therefore, we still need to develop these skills. To achieve the deepest levels of intimacy, we must be committed deeply to uncovering our old emotionally charged patterns.

Water coaches us to greater self-awareness through our relationships -- our relationship to our self, to our inner child, and to others. Water shows us how to run clear, clean, emotional current, to learn to respond to life instead of reacting to it, to activate the power of love, to access the ecstatic level through play, to wash away old wounds to create space for the water in our bodies to hold a new vibration, and to actively program our inner Water with the power of love.

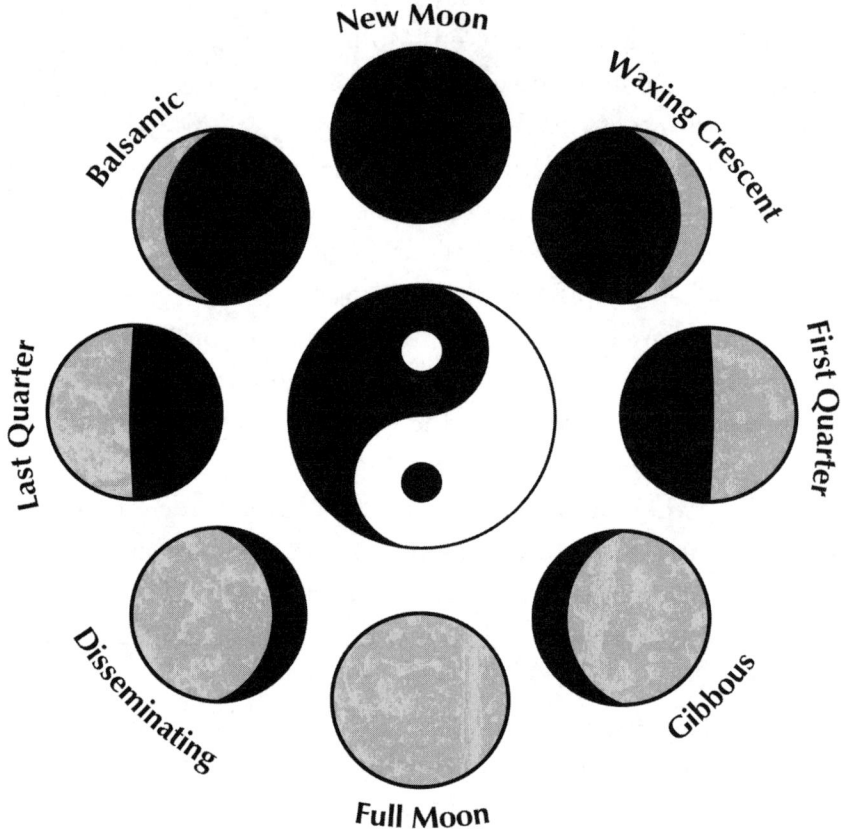

Natural Rhythm Cycle: Moon Phases

We become skilled at Water's power of ebb and flow through her natural rhythm -- the moon cycle -- as well as through our connection to both the outer world and our own inner landscape. As it does its sacred dance, the moon follows the same rhythmic pattern as the sun, also creating the yin/yang symbol. The new moon begins the expanding phase of the cycle. Just as the light expands in the Wheel of the Year from Winter Solstice until its peak at the Summer Solstice, the moon grows until it reaches its peak at the full moon. The expanding phase of the moon cycle is called waxing.

The contracting and releasing phase of the cycle from the full moon back to the new moon is called waning. Since the pattern mimics that of the sun, each of the moon's phase points also corresponds to a point on the Wheel of the Year.

 ***New Moon*** - This point of the monthly cycle begins the rebirth time of the light of the moon and corresponds to the yearly birth of the light of the sun at Winter Solstice. Here we plant the seeds we want to grow during this expanding phase. During the dark time of the moon directly preceding this phase, we want to do the deep inner reflection necessary to gain clarity around the seeds we want to bring forth.

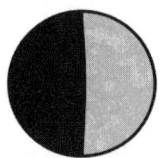 ***Waxing Crescent*** - Just as at Imbolc, the seedlings of our intentions are tender shoots in this phase. Here we ask what our seedling intentions need to grow fully -- more Water or love? more focus with Air? more grounding for Earth? or perhaps more life force from Fire?

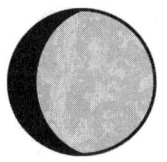 ***First Quarter*** - This is the moon's time of balance, and corresponds to Spring Equinox. Since, the growing phase of the cycle is half over, we can now take action to push toward fulfilling the intentions planted at the new moon phase.

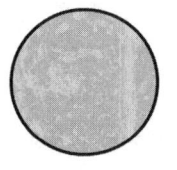 ***Gibbous*** - The moon's energy now starts to feel full, and we may begin to feel the pressure to complete what we began creating. The time has come to hold our focus and to actively work with the energy of our creations. This phase corresponds to Beltane.

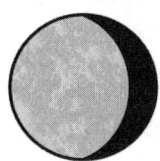 ***Full Moon*** - The energy of this monthly point is ripe and full, just like the yearly point of Summer Solstice. The intensity of this phase shows us what we have achieved. We see here how well we held and worked with our intention. The time has come for gratitude and reflection. How well have we done with our creations? What may we need to alter in the next cycle?

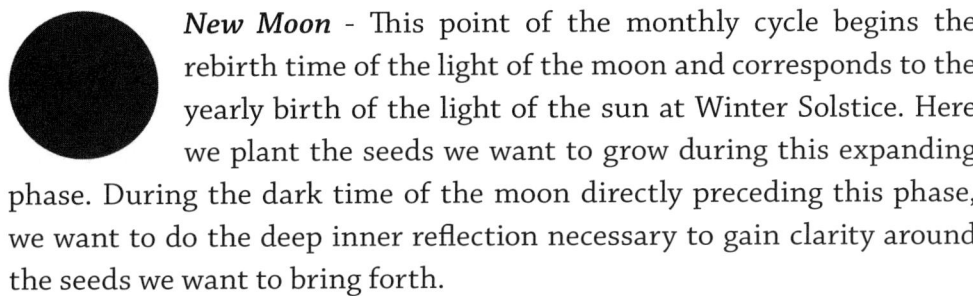 ***Disseminating*** - During this part of the cycle, we want to begin looking emotionally at what occurred during the growing phase. Depending on how much we accomplished or what we created, we may be able to joyfully pick the fruit of

the growing cycle, just as we do at the first harvest festival of Lughnasad. Additionally, we may need to reexamine our process.

Last Quarter - As the cycle comes to a close, we need to take time for inner work. What thoughts, beliefs, emotions, or patterns might we release at this time? The time has not quite arrived to begin the next cycle, nor is this cycle completely over. Like Autumnal Equinox, it is time to tune into what we can do in the inner realm to create more fertile soil for our next planting season.

Balsamic - This final stage of the monthly cycle, like Samhain, begins the dark phase. This serves as the time for deep inner rest and renewal, as well as the period to reflect upon what is coming to the surface of our awareness to bring forth during the next cycle.

A woman's menstruation cycle shares similarities in both consciousness and rhythm to the moon's cycle. In consciousness, a menstruating woman feels fresh and new after her menses, much like a new moon. From this portion of her cycle through to ovulation, much like a full moon, she has energy for the outside world and to work on manifesting her dreams. Once ovulation occurs, she begins the reflective journey into herself. This inner journey often calls for a time of retreat from so much outer-world activity. Women need time to attend to their emotional realm monthly to stay clean, clear, and current. They need to go within to examine and release what they no longer need from their emotional body and to bring their dreams out from the deep source of creation found at their core.

This natural cycle of outwardly connecting to others and to external activity, and then, turning inward for quiet and reflection is essential to a woman's inner balance. If a woman falls out of sync or harmony with this natural feminine rhythm, she may suffer from premenstrual syndrome (PMS), moodiness, depression, disconnection from her feelings, or frustration with herself for being unable to function in an outer-world-clock and calendar-oriented environment. Even a small block of time carved out of a woman's busy schedule, and designed solely for her to attend to her emotional well-being, can make a tremendous difference in her ability to thrive in life.

Additional Water Mystery School Teachings

Dive Deep

Water teaches us to dive to the depths of our feeling realm to get to the bottom of our emotions. It takes courage to allow ourselves to feel fully and to explore our feelings, looking and experiencing what lies at the bottom of our emotions not just on the surface. Our feelings may be so deep -- and so old -- that they are part of our cellular make-up, actually existing from the time we were born. Perhaps we possess feelings developed in childhood that we need to remember and heal. Even if the emotions are old, we can clear them if we allow ourselves to fully feel them.

Many people were taught not to feel some of their most intense feelings, such as fear, anger, rage, grief, jealousy. Yet in the expression of those feelings we can find some of our deepest healing. We need to become aware of what part of us feels those emotions and allow ourselves to connect to them, to feel them in order to resolve some of our core issues. Diving deep emotionally takes courage -- the courage to look beyond the surface of our feelings and to explore the depth of our emotions.

Exercise: Feeling Deeply

The next time you notice you are feeling a strong emotion, as soon as possible allow yourself time and space to fully feel it. Ask the feeling to show you what lies at the bottom of that feeling, and see what emerges in your consciousness. Water may take you through layers of feelings before you reach what lies at the depths. The more you can feel fully each layer of emotion, the more you can move the energy associated with it. You may discover more insight if you journal about the feeling.

Ebb and Flow

The moon's connection to water teaches us about ebb and flow through her pull on the tides and through her cycle of change. The moon changes as she goes through the cycle of light and dark each month, paralleling the principle that the sun teaches us in the night and day cycle and, as previously mentioned, through the Wheel of the Year. The moon also affects the element of Water through her cyclic pull on the tides. Working with the moon and Water, we are reminded again that life has a rhythm -- a time to move outward, forward, embrace; and a time to move inward, reflect, release.

The new moon is the seeding time for our desires and offers us the energy of outward movement and growth that comes during the weeks before the full moon, the waxing cycle. Then during the weeks from the full moon back to the new moon again, we turn within to be with our inner awareness during the waning cycle.

The moon's pull to create Water's rhythmic dance of moving in and out from the shore teaches us about the times to embrace others and the times to move more deeply into ourselves -- about the times to give and the times to receive. When we polarize ourselves with one primary way of being, such as always embracing others and giving of ourselves and to others, we sometimes give so much that nothing is left for us to draw upon internally. We must make time to receive from others as well as connect to our inner awareness and growth. When we learn to dance with the rhythmic ebb and flow of life, our relationship to every facet of our life improves. We allow ourselves to live in harmony with the organic flow of nature.

Emotional Awareness

As our emotional awareness develops, our capacity to be in the natural flow of nature increases. Connecting to how we feel in any given moment and acknowledging that awareness can lead us to more fully understand our emotional rhythms. This, in turn, allows us to work with those rhythms to bring our desires into being. However, for our creations and desires to come into form, Water and our emotions need to be in alignment with the other elements.

When we tune into our feelings and listen to what they tell us about our lives, we learn to recognize when our emotions have become imbalanced, excessive, or blocked in some way. If we block or try to stop a feeling from moving fully through our body, it gets trapped and stuck somewhere in the body. Trapped emotions and feelings can sometimes lead to stiffness in the body or muscles, illness, or a feeling of blockage, lack of flow, or non-movement somewhere in our lives. We may have learned in childhood to bury or repress our feelings, and we now have to practice to uncover and fully feel them.

When our Water realm is felt fully and clearly, we can use it to enhance and nourish our creations. Because the body contains our personal water, to increase our understanding of our feelings, and the body sensations that those feelings manifest, we need to place our awareness in our body. Increasing emotional awareness is an important step in developing emotional maturity.

Emotional Support & Safety

The more we feel emotionally supported and safe, the greater becomes our potential to flourish and grow. This sense of emotional support and safety gives us an emotional base from which to take risks, express who we are, love deeply, and extend emotional support to others. It offers us a springboard for our inner development.

Some people experienced this level of support from their families while they were growing up, but others who did not, must find a way to develop and give it to themselves as adults. We give ourselves emotional support and safety when we honor all of our feelings, when we trust in our ability to bring forth our dreams and desires, and when we talk kindly to ourselves, express self love, learn to see the perfection in our imperfection, and practice self-forgiveness. Our emotional stability helps us feel comfortable enough to express who we are and to share our vulnerability with others.

Feeling Guidance

Feelings carry a tremendous ability to guide our actions. For this reason, we want to listen to how we really feel about something instead of just following our head, or the crowd, or simply repeating old habits. We also want to learn when we are responding to our inner feelings, and when we are reacting to them. A reaction frequently is based on fear and can send us off in a different direction than we might choose if we listened to our feelings as guidance and responded accordingly.

The more conscious we become about letting our feelings guide us, the clearer our emotional Water becomes. If we aren't practiced at feeling our emotions, initially expressing our emotions may seem strange, perhaps even a little frightening. Yet, as with all the others, mastering the emotional realm will help us with our overall life development and guidance.

Only when we feel all our emotions can our feelings deeply guide us. Some people habitually only acknowledge "positive" feelings and ignore other signals and guides from their bodies and life. However, those feelings we call "negative" have messages for us as well. For example, frustration could be a message that something in our life isn't working for us and we need to take action -- make a change or, perhaps clear an old feeling. Or our anger about a certain situation could indicate that we need to take better care of ourselves in that situation. With an awareness of our feelings, we can determine what in our life we want to put our energy into and where we want to make changes. We can know which people we want to spend time with and learn to be aware of the places we need to grow emotionally -- all from listening to and being aware of our feelings.

We feel things all the time, whether we are aware of these emotions or not. They come up in response to actual, or even imagined events. Joy, anger, sadness, grief, love, gratitude -- a vast array of feelings could be running through your body at any moment. Feelings add richness and quality to our lives. Without feelings, we harden and wither like a plant that isn't watered. Deep feelings or very powerful feelings can cause us to feel like we are drowning in our emotions. It takes practice fully feeling our emotions and allowing them to flow completely through our bodies for us to feel comfortable with this experience. In actuality, when we allow ourselves to completely feel them, they move through us fairly quickly and with practice we become much more comfortable with them.

Float

Water's ability to float teaches us to trust the buoyancy of this fluid substance. Learning to float requires us to let go and relax into simply being supported. Our lives flow with more ease when we allow Water and our feelings to hold us afloat and to sustain us. When we release into this emotional state, our lives feel effortless and fluid.

Holding Space

Holding space represents the ability to maintain an internal place of openness and energy into which awareness can move. When we hold space for someone or something, it means we create in our consciousness the container for that person or thing to unfold. We simply intend, believe, and envision that Spirit is flowing through the person or situation. When we hold space we don't need to fix or rescue another person. We simply trust that their experiences are part of their evolutionary path.

When we hold emotional space for others, we listen to and receive what they are communicating without judgment. We allow space for whatever is happening within them, and we help that energy move freely by not adding our opinion, only receiving what they are saying. We can reflect back to them what we heard them saying, without adding our spin on it; we don't judge it or interpret it, but simply acknowledge or repeat what they said so they know they were heard. This allows someone to release what needs to be released without emotional engagement on the listener's part. This is a very powerful relationship tool to use with others, as well as for ourselves.

Nourishment

Water, an essential nutrient, sustains life. Land, plants, and people wither and die when they go too long without water. Drinking lots of water especially nourishes the physical body. Emotionally, feeling and giving appreciation provides one of the best ways to nourish yourself and others. The rich energy of true appreciation gives an uplifting gift to the soul and to the spirit. Everything is nourished when we give it appreciation -- children, land, homes, partners, jobs, bodies -- even Water itself.

Pace

Water teaches us about pace with its winding lazy rivers, still lakes, rushing waterfalls, calm oceans, and tidal waves. Sometimes water runs slow and lazy and other times rushes wildly. Our emotions follow a similar pattern. Sometimes, when our emotional response to life is slow and well-paced, navigating life seems like rowing on a calm lake. Other times, our emotional current is intense, and we feel engulfed by the ocean. As we begin to understand its pace, Water urges us to be with the emotional energy that moves through us at any given time and to learn to go with the flow of that movement. Water teaches us to work with our feelings and emotions in different settings, environments, and energy.

Play

Most of us learn Water's ecstatic realm of play early in our lives as we run under the water hose, swim in the pool, splash at the seashore, float in the lake, or delight in a bathtub full of bubbles. Keeping play alive in our lives helps us find the energy to do our work in the world and fill ourselves with joy. Many adults could use a good dose of Water's ecstatic realm of play and the fun it brings to their lives. Go splash at the next possible opportunity!

Regeneration

Regeneration occurs when Water re-fills our empty emotional container with the juice for life. When we regenerate, we don't just rest, we allow ourselves to be fully renewed. Water is the element of regeneration, of complete recharging. When we spend time in or near water and ask it to regenerate us, we receive an infusion of healing, health, and zest for life.

Relationship with the Inner Child

Within us lives the child we were at all ages and stages of development. In adulthood, it is our job to parent our inner child aspect, to listen to it, to love it, and to nurture it. Occasionally, we may bump up against a childhood emotion that needs clearing. We may have had a trauma as a child that our adult self thinks we have already handled and moved beyond; yet our inner child feels unable to move past this experience until we do some deep emotional clearing. Learning to honor and to listen to the inner child helps us develop emotional clarity and maturity.

Our inner child still carries our childhood dreams, passions, joys, wounds, and fears. As such, this aspect of ourselves can help us remember our deepest essence of self. It can help us remember the things we love to do and what makes us feel most alive.

Sometimes our inner child may need to be lovingly coached out from years of neglect and lack of attention. If we suffered physical or emotional abuse during childhood, we will need to address those deeply held memories and traumas to fully reclaim the spirit-filled child that also lives within.

If we treat ourselves harshly, demanding more of ourselves than appropriate, our inner child may retreat and become silent, and then may need gentle coaxing to come forth and share feelings and guidance. As we continue learning to love, hold, nurture, listen to, and play with our inner child, we make way for the gifts they bring to our life.

Exercise: Inner Child Dialogue

Dialoguing with your inner child provides a wonderful technique for learning about this aspect of yourself. Start by asking your inner child a question. Use one color ink to write down a question for your inner child with your dominant hand. Then, answer the question using a different color pen and your non-dominant hand. It can take a long time to write with your non-dominant hand, and it may feel difficult, but the wait and the effort are worth it. When I write with my non-dominant hand, my handwriting looks so much like the writing of my childhood. By using this process, I have discovered so much about how my inner world is working at any given point in time. So get out your journal soon, and try asking your inner child questions like: How are you? Is there something you need to tell me? You might be surprised by the answers you get.[8]

Relationship to Self

As we journey from the Water teachings of the inner child to the next level of emotional development, we arrive at the area of self-esteem or self-worth -- our relationship to our self. We discover that what we feel about our self is one of the most important aspects of our lives and one of Water's primary teachings.

In fact, our relationship with ourselves represents the most important relationship we have in life, because this relationship determines our level of self-esteem. With low self-esteem, life may seem hard and difficult. When love, regard, and respect for self increases, our perception of our life improves. Thus, with high self-esteem, we are better able to uplift and enjoy our life.

Every facet of life reflects the way we feel about ourselves. In particular, if we don't feel comfortable or good about ourselves, we won't try new things or take risks. This behavior may show up in subtle ways that we have held ourselves back, such as not taking steps to achieve a dream we have had or by keeping ourselves out of a relationship we have desired. Indeed we are not supporting ourselves in getting what we desire in life.

It is important to become conscious of our deep beliefs about ourselves, because these beliefs affect our sense of self worth, and that sense of self worth affects everything we do, touch, feel, see, experience, and become. It affects every way we behave in life and everything we achieve.

Increasing our awareness of how we feel about ourselves takes diligent attendance to the feelings that come up about ourselves in day-to-day life. Even when we are thinking positively about life, we can have an under-current of another energy running through our emotional body. Most often, this under-current consists of a stream of emotions from childhood -- old trapped childhood feelings of shame, inadequacy, abandonment, resentment, or grief relating to how we feel about ourselves -- that still need clearing. Unless we have had support working with such childhood emotions, these old unfelt emotions may still be at the deepest depths of our emotional realm. Becoming sensitive enough to our emotional realm to work with and clear those deep feelings can provide us with a powerful tool for increasing our love of self.

Exercise: Self-Appreciation

Working with appreciation provides one way to practice loving yourself. In your journal, every day, write down ten things you love about yourself. Keep writing ten things every day until you've listed 360 attributes. This turns your view of yourself around 360 degrees and uplifts you in the process. It may seem like a simple exercise, but it has a profoundly transforming effect. Try this exercise and see for yourself. The loving attributes you list can be as simple as you chose. Just keep going until you complete all 360. When you finish, treat yourself to something you have wanted for a long time, such as: a massage, a beautiful new outfit or time in nature -- something that makes you feel wonderful.[9]

Relationship to Others

As our self-esteem increases and we learn to respond to situations instead of reacting to them emotionally, Water takes us to the next layer of development, our relationships with others. At this point, we will begin practicing staying connected to our own inner essence while also staying connected to other people.

Water mirrors back to us our beliefs and emotional patterns through our relationships to others. This mirror serves as Water's main tool for teaching us about ourselves. Opening to see Water's true nature, its ability to mirror, is essential for increasing our emotional awareness. We can gain the perspective necessary for Water to teach us fully when we trust that what we see and experience mirrors something within us. As long as we hang on to the belief that our old view is "right," Water has no chance to show us the truth of the situation, or to help us mature and grow.

If we can surrender to the revelation shown to us in the looking glass of Water, we truly can see what judgments, beliefs, and thoughts we hold about our world. We can see what we have rejected inside ourselves and, in turn, projected outside of ourselves. For example, if we don't express anger ourselves, we might attract angry people into our lives to experience this emotion for us. If we have judgment of ourselves, we might attract people to criticize us. Whenever we have an emotional charge or judgment -- expressed or unexpressed, our emotional energy goes toward that and draws it to us in some way, shape, or form.

Water will show us the truth of relationship confusion or conflict if we have the courage to look in the mirror and see ourselves as part of the situation. Water reminds us that in every situation we remain the lens through which we perceive the world. We cannot see or know anything without it going through our filters. When we commit to emotional growth work, we clean our inner filters or lenses, and our relationships clear and change. Water teaches us through the mirror of relationships because we find it easier to see with clarity that which lies outside of us than that which resides inside us. When we learn to see our relationships as teachers, we take a giant step toward the development of emotional maturity, and our relationships often improve tremendously.

Emotional balance makes up an important component of our relationships with others. When we achieve emotional balance, we value our time, energy, talent, and worth to their full extent, and our relationships balance more easily. When we over give of or undervalue ourselves in some way, achieving balance in our relationships becomes more difficult. When we are in old emotional patterns, we sometimes expect the balance of giving and receiving to happen naturally. The old teaching that it is better to give than to receive only leads to imbalanced relationships. It is important to learn to do both. Learn to receive as well as to give. Our job involves making sure we are honored appropriately and don't give ourselves away totally to a relationship, job, or cause where an inappropriate or uneven exchange of energy exists. Peruvians call the balance of energy in an exchange *anyi*.[10] *Anyi* needs to be balanced in our exchanges with others for us to have a good sense of self-worth.

To notice when a relationship situation is balanced or not, we may have to tune into our feelings in unaccustomed ways. Our feelings point the way and guide us to right action and relationship if we allow them to do so. When we balance receiving and giving, we maintain our emotional balance.

Surrender

Water has a famous saying: "Go with the flow." This element teaches us this by having us let go of the shore to learn to swim, to float, and to travel down the stream of life. Water teaches us that sometimes we have to release control of forcing circumstances, events, or people to meet our expectations, and simply surrender to the lessons of the emotional realm. Trust lies at the core of our ability to surrender to the journey of our lives. It comes from a deep inner knowing that all that we are experiencing evolves from our soul's learning process.

Sweet Water, with deep gratitude we thank you
for quenching our thirst, for love, and for nurturing our hearts
and souls. Bless you for your guidance in our relationships and
emotional development. We are grateful to you for nourishing
all that grows in our lives.

CHAPTER FIVE

Air

"Human beings, vegetables, or cosmic dust,

we all dance to a mysterious tune intoned

in the distance by an invisible player."

Albert Einstein

Air

Mental Realm

Mystery School Teachings:
Sacred geometry, intention, meditation, conscious language, prayer, vibration, crystals, sound, color.

Developmental Task:
Consciously set your vibrational tone

Key Word: Visionary

Soul Quality: Peace

Ecstatic Realm: Soaring

Primary Power: Intention

Level 2 Power: Focus

Natural Rhythm Cycle: Astrology Wheel

*S*ound, tone, and vibration all travel on the airwaves, the invisible transmitter. Even though we can't see it, we feel Air's effects when it warms us on a hot summer day or chills us to the bone when it blows in the middle of winter. Lack of air, for even a minute, can damage our brains and bodies for the rest of our lives. We constantly take air into our bodies and the fresher air we take in the better. Stale air with an unappealing odor repels us, and smog or air pollution is dangerous to our health. We need a supply of fresh clean air to fully feel alive and vital.

The same holds true in our consciousness, the area governed by the element of Air. Just as we need clean air to breathe, we need a clean mental realm that can focus clearly on our intent and help us maintain a powerful perspective from which to vision our lives. In relation to the other elements, Air moves fast and is not easily contained. Mental chatter easily clutters up our minds. We need our mental realm free from chatter, worry, and negative thought for it to function at its optimal capacity. The Air realm can teach us to clear our old mental patterns and to focus on our desires.

Despite its invisibility, Air is an extremely powerful element in our lives. Quite literally, without it we no longer exist in this realm. Seeing a baby take his or her first breath of life, or being with someone as they take their last breath, we more deeply understand the powerful impact of this mysterious substance. None of us can go very long without our next breath. Breath fills our lungs, our brain, and every cell in our body with its enlivening essence.

Air also helps us experience life from a variety of perspectives as it moves from person to person and place-to-place in its circulating dance. We may be breathing the air that someone across the state was breathing a while ago. Not only do we share air, we also share airwaves and all that travels on them. If we tune in, we can access the thoughts of others through the Air realm as they travel from person to person. This is where we access our telepathic, intuitive, psychic, and clairvoyant abilities. The airwaves hold the universal thought sphere, which some people call the "collective consciousness." This explains why each of us increasing our own personal vibration and awareness affects the collective -- the people in our communities, countries, and world -- grow in consciousness.

The elemental mystery school of Air includes the mental realm and all its many functions. It contains many tools to aid in its teachings and for its attunement, such as: conscious thought, conscious language, right and left brain integration, working with a unified field, balance, prayer, meditation, intention, setting a vibration, vibrational healing techniques, sound, smell, light, vision, sacred geometry, clairvoyance, intuition, communication, astrology, and etheric guides. Air works as a vast and powerful realm.

Air Skills and Powers

The first Air skill we need is the ability to listen to the inner guidance we receive constantly, to what the world around us says, and to what the wind whispers when it blows through the trees. Even those who are deaf can listen to the messages that come from within, from the world around them, or from the sacred voice of nature.

Our ability to listen brings us to the center of our lives, the still focused place of awareness. From there we can be guided toward our most effective next steps in life and toward wholeness, health, relationships, work, and spiritual growth. We need to listen to the voice of Spirit guiding us and also follow its guidance. We must learn to discern the voice of our inner spirit's guidance from the voice of our ego self. They have different qualities and often the ego argues with the spirit self as it guides us. If we cannot discern the difference in their voices, we may find it difficult to hear the voice of our spirit when it speaks.

Our spirit guidance may tell us to put a favorite ring away while our ego self tells us the ring will be fine, and then the ring gets lost. Or perhaps our spirit self says it is not in our best interest to move and the ego self tells us a change of location will work out fine, but when we make the move we realize the step was inopportune. While we may have lived through the loss of the ring and the inopportune move, and learned deeply from our choices, in the process we developed the muscle of fine-tuning our inner listening so we learn when we are following guidance from Spirit, which has a different energetic quality to it, and when we are not.

The next layer of listening development comes from noticing the Air realm's effect on the element of Water. When we hear something externally, or someone says something directly to us, or we hear it broadcast on the airwaves, we might either react or respond. It takes a deep level of inner awareness to notice what thoughts and feelings arise when we hear things over the airwaves. Do we react by going into fear when certain types of information are pumped out through the media, such as on the radio or television? Can we choose to respond with feelings of love and peace even when we are bombarded with messages carrying negativity and fear? Air teaches us to hold our vibration and emotional balance as we interact with the world.

Air influences our Water realm, because we use it to program Water. In much the same way, our thoughts and belief systems deeply affect the emotions we hold and feel. As we work with the interaction of these two elemental realms, Air and Water, we come to the developmental stage of aligning them fully. In actuality we are aligning head and heart. Working separately, they can have us swinging from one aspect of life to another. Our head wants to do this and our heart that. When aligned, we can make choices that consider both realms fully and take integrated steps toward our desires.

This alignment of head and heart helps us integrate intellect and intuition as well. Again, one without the other only provides part of the picture, but together they offer the richness of multiple ways of knowing, which we then have at our disposal. From this unified place of head/heart and intellect/intuition, and with our deep inner listening ability, which is enhanced by their alignment, our dreams and desires come more clearly into focus, and we can begin activating the powers of Air.

Air brings us the primary power of intention and the level two power of focus. Our intention helps us define both our purpose for doing something and the end result we desire. The defining power of Air gives us the directional focus toward our co-creations. We use intention for creating inner-world growth as well as for setting and achieving our outer-world goals. Setting intentions is like setting the target of our desires so we know our aim. We don't always need to know how we will get where we are going, we just need to know where we are heading.

Sometimes, we may find ourselves in the midst of a life transition, a time of deep change, and not know consciously what is coming next. At those times, even when we don't know where we are going we can focus our mental attention in a constructive manner. We can have the intention to be present in the unknown until the next step is revealed to us.

For our intention to come into form fully, we also need commitment. Commitment is the energy that helps us see something through until completion. It works hand in hand with the level two power of Air -- focus. If we are committed to our intention, focus helps us realign when we get off track. We have so many choices in life, so many places to put our energy, so many interesting things to explore and people to meet. Focus helps us keep directing our attention towards our desires until they fully come into form.

When we try to bring everything into form at once, the energy, the creational juice, gets too dispersed. When we focus on one creation at a time, we generate enough concentrated power to bring a desire into form. We are gifted with the ability to think and to be discriminating in the focus of our thoughts. Focusing our attention on anything amplifies its energy, so we need to be sure to keep our focus on what we desire in life. What we focus on expands.

This concept represents a critical Air tool. If we focus on what we don't want or have, we simply get more of that. Turning our attention back to what we do want sometimes requires a subtle shift, but a highly important one just the same. To achieve this shift, we must begin noticing our thoughts and words. If we observe ourselves thinking or saying that we don't know what we want, but we know what we don't want, we need to discover our desire then turn our attention toward that. While it is extremely important for us to keep our mental realm focused on what we choose to bring into being, we must simultaneously release any attachment to the outcome. Focusing our energy does not equate to controlling a situation.

To come fully into being, sometimes our creations have to move in ways we can not anticipate. Many times when we release control of a situation, Spirit and our guides move things into place that help us clear what is in the way of bringing the creation into being. We may need to uncover and release old belief systems or emotional baggage before the desire can come fully into form. If we struggle, control, or resist what is moving in our lives, we just might miss the lessons we are meant to learn and block the dream from becoming reality. We need to practice continually bringing our focus back to our intention.

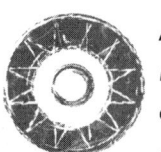

Activation: Air's Primary Power of Intention

Intention serves as Air's primary power tool. A strong, clear intention creates an effective mental container in which a desire can come to life. Actively setting an intention before starting something new helps us fully define our desires.

Preferably, do this exercise standing. If for any reason you cannot stand, your intention will work to activate the power while you remain seated. Find a great piece of music that feels powerfully Air-connected to you. Before putting on the music, state your intention out loud or silently in your head, to activate Air's power of intention. Place your awareness in your body; then put on your music and dance to activate, enliven, and embody your intention. Once complete with the dance, put your awareness in your body, and ask Air what else you need to know about the power of intention. Then listen internally for the answer to your question, and journal about the response you receive.

Exercise: Setting Intention

Intentions need to be clear, simply stated, and focused solely on the desired outcome, on what you desire, not what you no longer want or what you choose to release. In other words, saying, "My intention is to grow a garden free of any pests or weeds" puts the energy and focus on the pests and weeds. A more effective way of stating your intention might be, "My intention is to grow a beautiful, easy to maintain garden." Feel the difference in those two intentions.

An intention statement is a declaration of what you intend to activate in your life. For it to achieve the highest outcome, your intentions need to be stated in the most uplifting way possible, but you don't need to make it complicated. Keep the statement simple. A statement of intent works on a very deep level of consciousness. Choose something you would like to have come into being in your life and write an intention statement for it. Notice the movement of energy toward your intent. As you strongly set an intention, what actually shows up in your life at first may not look like the intention coming into form at all. Sometimes you need to flush out of your life anything less than the desired intent, meaning the old patterns you have been holding.

As you continue to focus upon your desire coming into form and aligning it with your feelings and actions, the more that desire will take shape and appear in your life. Remember, intention possesses the power of Air, and through it the tone and vibration of your life gets set. The clearer your intention for what you choose to create, the stronger and perhaps quicker your desires will come forth.

Exercise: Clearing the Mental Realm

Do this exercise when you need to focus or have a breath of fresh energy in your life. Perhaps you need fresh mental energy or focus for a job you are doing, or a clear mind for a relationship discussion. If so, Air can assist you. Sit in a quiet location and take a few deep breaths. Ask Air to tell you what you need to clear in order to focus your mind and have fresh mental energy. Now take a few deep breaths while asking to release what is no longer needed. Then open to receive a greater level of focus and clarity.

Exercise: Creating with Air

Air's creational tools work with anything formed with sounds or words. You can write a song about what you desire and sing it. Write or tell a story about the thing you most want to honor. Make music with any instrument. Write music, or use your voice to tone. Even creating a visual work of art using words or colors, such as a collage, allows Air to support you creatively. Choose something in your life you want to honor, express, or bring into being. An example might be honoring a major life passage, such as turning 20, 30, 40, 50, 60, 70, or 80. Next, decide what Air expression you would like to use to honor this event. Then creatively express it. Sing a song about turning sixty. Create a collage to show gratitude for your first thirty years of life. Write a creative story that describes what you want the next years of your life to look like. Have fun using one of Air's most precious tools -- your imagination.

Activation: Air's Level Two Power of Focus

Preferably, do this exercise standing. If for any reason you cannot stand, your intention will work to activate the power of focus while you are seated. Find a piece of music that feels good to you for activating focus. Before putting on the music, state your intention out loud or silently in your head, to activate Air's power of focus. Place your awareness in your body; then, put on your music and dance to activate, enliven, and embody the power of focus. Once complete with the dance, put your awareness in your body, and ask Air what else you need to know to more fully utilize the power of focus in your life. Then listen internally for the answer, and journal about the response you receive. Remember: whatever you focus on expands!

Exercise: Alignment of Head, Heart, Intellect and Intuition

Preferably, do this exercise standing. If for any reason you cannot stand, your intention will work to activate the alignment while you are seated. Find a great piece of music that feels appropriate to you for this alignment. Before putting on the music, state your intention out loud or silently in your head to align both your head and heart and your intellect and intuition. You can do both of these alignments to one song or separate them into two. If you dance to two different songs, take the time to journal after each one. Place your awareness in your body and actively call forth your head and heart and/or intellect and intuition. State your intent for alignment; then, put on your music, and dance to activate your alignment. Once complete with the dance, put your awareness in your body, and ask Air what else you need to know about working with these two aspects simultaneously. Then listen internally for an answer and journal about the response you receive.

Air's Developmental Task

Consciously setting our vibrational tone helps us create quality of life. Most of us only want our highest and best thought patterns to actually manifest in our lives. To accomplish this, we must learn to enhance our ability to think those kinds of thoughts and to discern what our lives are showing us about our belief systems and old emotional baggage. Simple changes in the way we view, think, and speak about our lives can alter remarkably the vibrational tone of our lives and assist us in manifesting our hearts' desires. When we can unwaveringly hold a desire clearly in our consciousness, regardless of what things look like externally, the more able we become to consciously create that desire.

From our first breath to our last, our words and vibrations set an individual tone that creates our lives and moves the matter of our lives. When that tone or vibration shifts, the matter of our lives adjusts accordingly. Words posses tremendous power. Speaking or writing activates the vibration of the words used and imbues it with life force. Therefore, it is vitally important that we respect the power of words and know how to use them consciously. Our thoughts and belief system play a critical role in increasing the awareness of the tone and vibration of words, so we must become conscious of these, as well as the words we use.

Words, whether thought, spoken, or written create a vibrational frequency. When we speak, the words move past our vocal cords and Air adds a vibrational force that increases the strength of the manifestational and creational tone of those words.

Communication flows in a two-way interaction. Both the words and the energy with which the words are spoken, thought, or written moves through the air waves to the people receiving the communication. Then, both the words and the energy are received and pass through the lens of the receivers' perceptional belief system. We've all experienced the feeling vibration of someone speaking to us when they were expressing anger, sadness, sarcasm, caring, or love. We instinctively know the tone sent along with their words. We sense the same thing when we read someone's writing -- the feeling tone the writer had while writing. The tone or vibrational quality comes across on the page. The same holds true for our thoughts. They carry a frequency that others pick up, regardless of our choice to voice them or keep them to ourselves.

Learning to speak, write, and think in ways that enhance maximum effectiveness of our communication requires increasing our awareness of the impact of the words we use. Our choice of words makes a tremendous difference in the vibration we set up and emit. Despite the subtle difference in word choice, the impact in their vibration can be quite powerful. Notice, for example, the difference in the power of these two sentences: "I will try to find a new job that pays more." Or "I will find a new job that pays more." A tremendous difference exists between, "I will try" and "I will." The word "try" takes away the statement's power, leaving it weak and ineffective. The statement "I will" is strong, clear, to the point, and committed to action.[1]

Air teaches us to speak and communicate from a place of congruency and integrity, meaning and doing what we say. Keeping our word or consciously renegotiating commitments creates trust in our relationships with others, and in our relationship with ourselves. Air teaches us the fundamental skills required to communicate with integrity by speaking truthfully, clearly, and honoring our word.

Stories are told of yogis and sages throughout time who have had the ability to create instantly with the power of their speech, thoughts, and vibration. As we increase our ability to work consciously with the elemental forces, we strengthen our capacity to bring forth our desires into manifest form, and manifestation happens more quickly. Thus, it becomes increasingly imperative to understand how our underlying belief systems set up vibrations, and how those vibrations cause manifestation to occur in our lives. We need to learn how to bring our unconscious belief systems into alignment with our conscious dreams and desires, to accomplish Air's developmental task of consciously setting the vibrational tone for our life. Only when we make the unconscious conscious do we learn to tune our lives to our desired frequencies and to create our lives consciously.

Our thoughts are vibrations. They have power -- the power to create. Each thought is like a seed carrying potential substance into the realm of creation.[2] Often we grow up carrying the beliefs of our childhood world. Sometimes we don't realize the limiting nature of those beliefs. A belief, like "You have to work hard and sacrifice for what you get in life," sets a tone. A completely different vibration comes from the belief "All my needs and desires come to me effortlessly and easily," or "I create my life dreams with ease and grace."

Noticing the difference in our beliefs provides one way we can begin to work with consciously setting the tone of our lives. We also can start noticing when we feel enlivened and full of life and become conscious of what we are thinking and doing at that time. If our energy drops in some way, we can notice what we are participating in that lowers our vibration. We might even want to experiment by talking unkindly to ourselves for a few minutes to see how we feel afterwards. We might then communicate with ourselves in a way that is optimistic and loving, and notice what that does to our energy systems.

Deeply held beliefs get stored in the cells of our body, which explains how our vibrational patterns get set. To change our vibrational tone, we must change a belief on the mental level, as well as on a cellular level.

As an example of how this works, let me tell you about a lesson I learned from Air on this very concept. Over several years, I had shifted my mental belief system around the balance of giving and receiving. As I was growing up, I absorbed the message that giving was better than receiving. I believed it was okay to receive some; at the core of my cells, however, I believed I needed to give more than I received.

My cellular belief manifested into a broader belief that I had to make sure everyone else's needs were met before I could receive. I gave a lot of care to others over the years, because, in this belief system, somehow others always became my responsibility. Shifting this belief system presented an enormous challenge for me.

I began the process of working with my belief about divinity and began to include a Divine Feminine model to balance the Divine Masculine. In this paradigm of balance, receiving is balanced with giving, being with doing, and feminine with masculine. Just as Water teaches us about balance through flow, Air teaches us about balance through the very act of breathing. We must inhale and exhale to stay alive. One will not work without the other. Both states must exist; both activities must take place to sustain life. So, Air teaches us how to hold a balanced belief system inclusive of multiple ways of being.

Years passed, and my consciousness evolved to embrace a new way of perceiving the balance of life. However, I finally realized that, while my mental model had changed, my cellular structure still was vibrating to my old belief system that I needed to give more. And, as it always happens, my life continued to reflect my belief system back to me, even in the subtlest of ways.

While playing a board game, I offered to sell a deal I had drawn at a moderate price, which actually took the buyer to the next level of the game. He told me later he would have paid me everything he had to purchase that card and to get him to that next level. We both could have come out winners had I asked for more or allowed him to make me an offer. Instead, I had simply given him a "good deal."

As I pondered the situation for the next 24 hours, I realized that after any negotiations I had participated in during the last few years I had come out feeling like I hadn't asked for enough for myself. I felt I hadn't fully honored myself. At the time, I didn't understand what internal belief or issue had caused that to happen repeatedly. I did, however, begin to see that I was taking responsibility for everyone else's needs first and only giving to myself afterwards.

After experiencing the same lesson many times, I finally understood and uncovered my deeply held cellular belief -- a belief left over from the days of my childhood. I now have done the release work to take that cellular belief out of my body, thus shifting the vibration that I radiate out to the world, and I have seen vibrant results.

Exercise: Clearing Beliefs

You can do a cellular belief system clearing with Air by determining, to the degree you can at the time, the old belief that needs to be cleared. Sometimes, more than one belief is affecting things, and you may need to clear one and then clear a couple more. After you have identified the belief, out loud or silently state what you intend to clear from your cells. Such as, "I choose to clear the belief that I need to give more than receive." Now take a deep breath and blow the old belief out of your cellular structure as you blow the air out of your lungs. Notice how your body feels, and continue clearing until your body feels light and your energy feels open.

You can replace your old beliefs with beliefs of your choice, and it is important to choose and input the new belief. Such as, "I choose to balance giving and receiving in my life." Simply state your new beliefs and breathe in to anchor them. You can help fully embody the new belief by dancing it into being. State your intention, put on music, and dance to anchor the new belief in your physical body.

Exercise: Consciously Setting Your Vibrational Tone

Your vibrational tone needs to be set consciously. Making a daily habit of setting it will uplift your life tremendously. Consciously setting your vibrational tone works to help you create the quality of life you choose. Sit quietly in a meditative state. Take a few deep breaths. Ask Air to uplift your vibration to the highest-level possible, and breathe again. Ask to consciously connect to the Divine within and the frequency of love. Open to feel the influx of energy. Breathe until you feel the energy has filled your body. Ask the energy if it has any guidance for you. Ask that your vibrational tone be set here.

Natural Rhythm Cycle: Astrology Wheel

Both the sun and moon respond to the influence of stars as they pass through the zodiac or astrology wheel each month and year. The harmonic movement of these celestial bodies creates a pulse and rhythm. Together their movement creates a vibration called the music of the spheres. In turn, we respond vibrationally to the energy of their music and to the subtle changes it makes. The more we listen to the "uni-verse" and respond to the sacred beat and timing it plays, the more we become aligned in our sacred dance of life.

The 12 Gates of Awareness found in astrology -- Aries, Taurus, Gemini, Cancer, Leo, Virgo, Libra, Scorpio, Sagittarius, Capricorn, Aquarius, and Pisces -- each develop our consciousness in different ways and give us a natural rhythmic boost of energy to bring our dreams into reality. When we line up our creations with their natural flow and teachings, it becomes easier to bring things into form. These twelve astrological gates create subtle energy shifts every month and every year. The sun passes through the astrological gates every year and the moon each month. Aligning with the energy they bring makes a tremendous difference in the quality of our life.

Astrology is an ancient study with various interpretations. Each person who works with Astrology adds their own slant and perspective to it. Each of the twelve gates of awareness provides a different lens through which to interpret energy and offers an archetypal perspective from which we can learn. The organic teaching of these gates includes the belief that each perspective has validity and a place in the larger whole. We need to learn from these gates and to put the information they provide through our inner filters to discover what parts of their teachings ring true in our lives at a particular time. The archetypal energies will work with each of us personally to uncover the best way for us to use them in our lives.[3]

Astrology teaches us the dance of the cosmos through the rhythm of the sun, moon, stars and planets. Because of its vast skill set, astrology is best learned in layers or one step at a time before adding the next level of complexity. Like any layered learning process, we must apply time, interest, and both sides of our brain to the study. Our skill development happens both through the left-brain's ability to structure and sequence and our right brain's ability to creatively interpret the energies. Applying whole brain learning to our study of astrology gives us the most potential in our creational work.

To work with the 12 Gates of Awareness of astrology, we must begin with a basic understanding of each archetype. Once we feel like we know them to some degree, we can begin to work with them in relation to our knowledge of others and of self. Then we can apply the archetypes to the timing of our co-creations. For example, we can align with the sun and the moon and the astrological gate of awareness they are in when we are ready to bring one of our dreams into the world of form. This forms the beginning of our learning. If we become open to and interested in these archetypes and their energies, the layers of the vast and fascinating cosmic dance can bring us much life perspective.

Understanding the Twelve Archetypal Gates of Awareness

Each of the four elements divides itself into three different archetypes, which then comprise the 12 archetypes, often called "signs," of the Astrological Wheel. To work with each archetype or gate of awareness, we must first align ourselves with its element. Fire has its own way of functioning and its

Astrology Note:
Dates of the archetypes are based on Western Astrology and the dates vary slightly because of leap years.

unique properties, whether it is moving through Aries, Leo, or Sagittarius. Earth connects us to the physical realm in all three of its archetypes: Taurus, Virgo, or Capricorn. The Air signs, Gemini, Libra, and Aquarius, take us into the invisible mental realm. We dive into the emotional feeling realm with Water's divisions, Cancer, Scorpio, and Pisces. The element is the first thing to understand. If we first understand the element, then we can work with the different ways in which it expresses through each archetype.

In this book, we've explored how the elements work, by starting with the feminine axis of Earth and Water and then looking at the masculine axis of Air and Fire. We have followed the same path the teachings took as they came into being originally and as I have been taught to work with them. Astrologically, the wheel follows a somewhat different path. The first gate has us enter through Fire, the masculine sign of Aries and the initiating spark of life. We then travel around the wheel to a feminine Earth sign, a masculine Air sign, a feminine Water sign, and continue this pattern all the way around the wheel. In this manner, the wheel expresses the balance of the masculine and feminine throughout the sacred archetypal dance.

Aries, a fire sign, creates the first gate of awareness, teaching the meaning of individuation. An active, high spirited, and energetic archetype, Aries loves excitement, adventure, play, and competition. As a sacred warrior, it will fight to defend its beliefs and to protect what is young and growing. It likes to go first, to get things started, and to lead the way. Courageous, trusting, decisive, inspired, and spontaneous, Aries serves as the Fire point of the cross at Spring Equinox. The sun is generally in Aries from March 21- April 19.

Taurus, an Earth sign, creates the second gate of awareness, teaching the value of enjoying the earthly realm of matter. It delights in all that looks beautiful, tastes delicious, and feels pleasurable. It loves receiving all the exquisite things and gratifications the physical realm offers. It also knows how to take solid steps to attain its desire for possessions, wealth, and security. It connects to the Divine when it savors and enjoys intimacy through the body and senses. The sun is generally in Taurus from April 20- May 20.

Gemini, an Air sign, creates the third gate of awareness, teaching the importance of the mind and of ideas. It craves fresh experiences, chances to use its imagination, fun, games, and change. This versatile and curious archetype often plays the comedian and perpetual youth. Gemini enjoys expressing itself through writing, speaking, or connecting to the Divine Muse through its many creative pursuits. It likes to communicate, network, and bring news and information. The sun is generally in Gemini from May 21 - June 20.

Cancer, a Water sign, creates the fourth gate of awareness, teaching the meaning of nurturing. A devoted caregiver to family, friends, and projects, this archetype loves home and comfort in all aspects of life. Cancers connect to others as the loyal and caring mother/father type and sympathize with the vulnerability of others, while creating safe emotional space for what is tender, young, and growing. On the Wheel of the Year, Cancer serves as the Water point of the cross at Summer Solstice. The sun is generally in Cancer from June 21- July 22.

Leo, a Fire sign, creates the fifth gate of awareness, teaching the value of radiance. Using the key of self-love to turn up its own radiance, Leo knows that the brighter its light shines the more it inspires others. This archetype represents the natural leader, performer, director, or celebrity. Self-confident, dramatic, regal, openhearted, generous, creative, expansive, powerful, and outgoing, Leo loves to be center-stage as a leading player, celebrating and sharing its zest for life. The sun is generally in Leo from July 23 - August 22.

Virgo, an Earth sign, creates the sixth gate of awareness, teaching the significance of dedicated work. It understands and honors patterns, timing, rhythms, and cycles. It accesses the Priest/ess within to honor, through ceremony and ritual, the sacred in the natural world. Organized, practical, dependable, and productive, Virgo is known as a hard worker with a tremendous capacity for handling the details of the earthly realm. In addition, Virgo is dedicated to doing its sacred work by being in service to the world around it. The sun is generally in Virgo from August 23 - September 22.

Libra, an Air sign, creates the seventh gate of awareness, teaching the importance of balanced relationships. It has the capacity to see things from all sides, to honor each person's point of view, to balance opposites, to consider options, and to mediate well. This archetype creates safe space for valuing all the other gates of awareness. Cooperative social skills make Libra a good partner, host/ess, and companion. Relationship represents Libra's spiritual path, and on the Wheel of the Year it serves as the Air point of the cross at Autumnal Equinox. The sun is generally in Libra from September 23 - October 22.

Scorpio, a Water sign, creates the eighth gate of awareness, teaching the power of feelings. This archetype fully feels the complete range of emotions, from icy and frozen, to hot and steamy, and learns to master its response to them. Intense and passionate about discovering what lies well beneath the surface of current awareness, Scorpio travels to the depths of Water's realm connecting to Source, and using the treasures it discovers there for generating life-force in Self and in others. It possesses a potent intuitive sixth-sense and the ability to travel into other realms of consciousness. The sun is generally in Scorpio from October 23 - November 21.

Sagittarius, a Fire sign, creates the ninth gate of awareness, teaching the significance of expansion. This dynamic, outgoing, truth-seeking explorer constantly quests for expansion and growth by physically and energetically seeking out new ideas and territories. It brings its expanded awareness and discoveries back to share with others as a teacher of philosophy and evolving states of consciousness. Sagittarius passionately searches for the meaning of life through freedom, growth, and development. The sun is generally in Sagittarius from November 22 - December 21.

Capricorn, an Earth sign, creates the tenth gate of awareness, teaching the value of structure and form. This archetype exhibits the characteristics of administrator, mature adult, wise one, disciplined teacher, hard working leader, good provider, and practical businessperson. Ambitious, responsible, effective, efficient, and goal oriented, it brings new structures into earthly form. Capricorn creates structures and systems designed to last and support the generations to come. On the Wheel of the Year, this archetype serves as the Earth point of the cross at Winter Solstice. The sun is generally in Capricorn from December 22 - January 19.

Aquarius, an Air sign, creates the eleventh gate of awareness, teaching the importance of innovation. Unique, inventive, progressive, and original, this sign has a cosmic perspective on life and often brings radical new ideas to humanity. The detached, free-spirited visionary who explores unconventional territory, Aquarius is interested in helping the world become a better place through humanitarian ideals of love and truth. The sun is generally in Aquarius from January 20 - February 18.

Pisces, a Water sign, creates the twelfth gate of awareness, teaching the importance of a compassionate heart. This archetype feels the grief and suffering of humanity and responds with a loving caring heart that heals. Pisces serves the world by dreaming the visions of a peaceful planet and selflessly helping others create a better life. Deeply spiritual, intuitive, and psychic, it completely merges with humanity and the divine. The sun is generally in Pisces from February 19 - March 20.

We will explore how to use the gates for aligning our co-creations in the chapter titled "Sacred Timings".

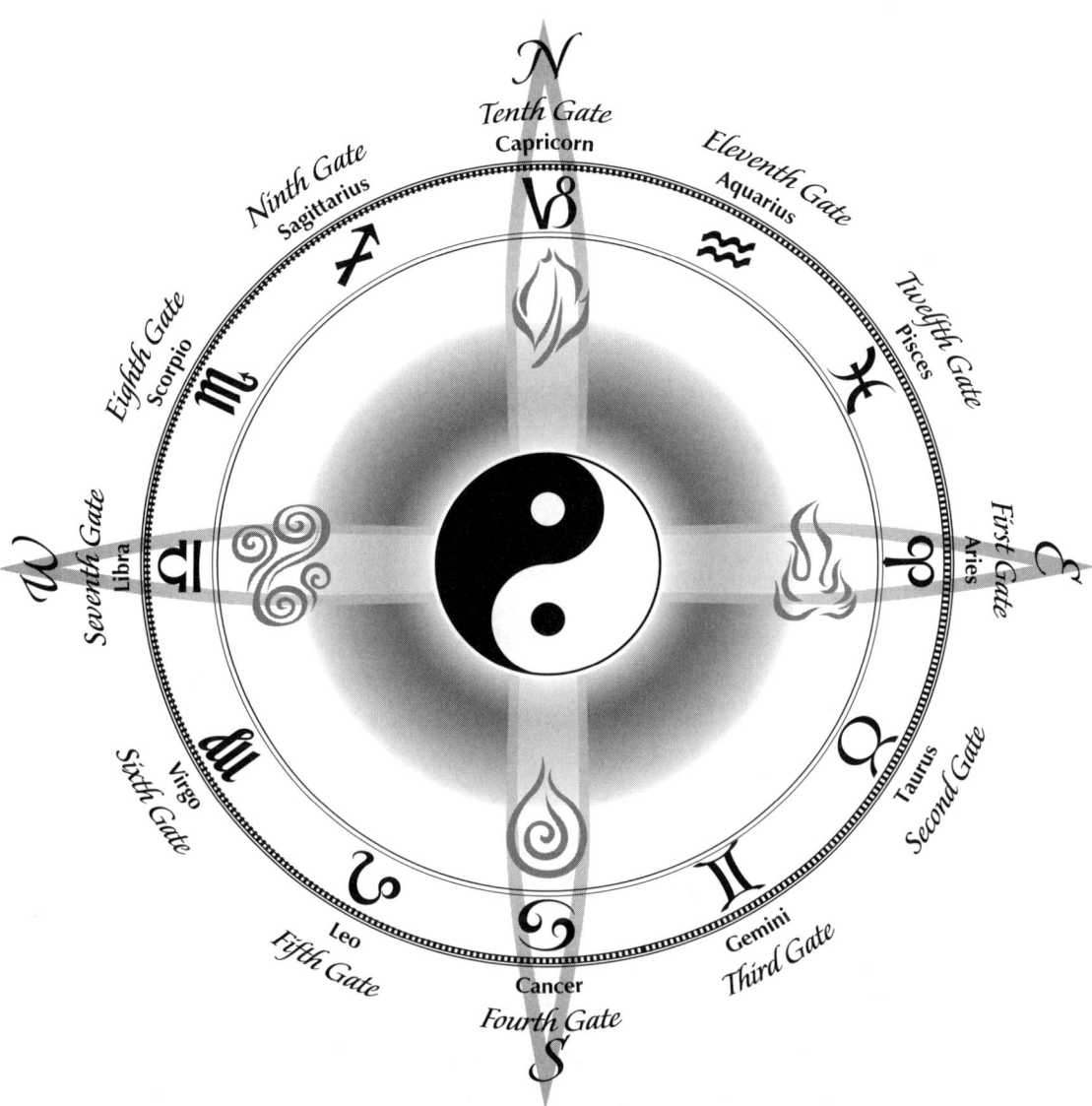

Dancer & Musical Note:
The twelve archetypes of astrology with the cross points as accents form 3/4 time.
1 (winter solstice) 2-3 / **2** (spring equinox) 2-3 / **3** (summer solstice) 2-3 / **4** (autumnal equinox) 2-3]

Additional Air Mystery School Teachings

Belief System

Our belief system acts as the lens through which we filter life. Throughout our lives, anything with which we come into contact is perceived through the lens of our belief system. How we interpret, think, and feel about everything we encounter arises out of our belief system. Our personal awareness increases as we examine our beliefs to determine if they were consciously chosen or unconsciously passed down to us. Each time we consciously choose our beliefs we increase our skill at setting the vibrational tone for our lives. Bringing our beliefs into conscious awareness increases our ability to use them as a mindful creational tool.

Air flows in and around all things and serves as the great connector of all the elemental forces. Since Air governs the realm of consciousness, what we believe connects all aspects of our lives and our experience.

Breath

The more conscious we are of our breathing and of fully filling our body with rich clean air, the more relaxed, energized, healthy, and alive we feel and become. Increasing our air intake makes a dramatic impact on our ability to think clearly and on the quality of our life. Wisdom keepers, sages, yogis, and athletes through the ages have explored the importance of conscious breathing to increase life force and to access altered states of awareness.

Communication

People think and communicate differently depending upon the element in which their thinking function lies. Some people are Earth communicators, some Water, some Air, and some Fire. Each person perceives, thinks, and communicates through the lens of their particular elemental style. Understanding the differences in these styles and being able to connect with elements different from our own can dramatically increase our ability to work, live, and communicate well with others.

Because communication flows as a two-way street between sender and receiver, the more we increase our consciousness as speakers and as listeners, the more successful our communications become. As speakers, the more we communicate in ways that all the elemental styles understand, the more effectively we send our messages. As listeners, the more we increase our receiving skills and our awareness of what happens within us when we hear something, the clearer becomes our responses to the messages we receive.

Ethereal Allies

Many people believe in unseen guides, teachers, angels, and allies. Working consciously with them can assist us tremendously in life. To bring this unseen help immediately to our side, we need only call internally for angelic guidance and assistance. We live on a planet that functions on the principle of free will. Therefore, we must ask for assistance or guidance before it can be given. Just know that the moment energy of any sort is called or invoked, it responds and honors our request.

The result of our requests for assistance may look different than we picture, however. So, stay open to the possibility that when we look at our circumstances in a larger-than-life perspective, they often have different meanings. Something we perceive as devastating in the moment may turn out to be our most powerful teacher or opportunity, and we may grow in tremendous ways because of that event. The more we allow the answering of our prayers to unfold, while staying open to Spirit's unseen working in our lives, the greater our capacity becomes for creating our dreams.

Energetic Cords

Uncleared energy with people or past situations can drain our creational life energy. Once cleared, that same energy becomes available to apply toward our creations. We can be corded energetically to people in our lives and also connected to a previous time in our own lives. When our minds continue to go back to a point in the past connected to a person or a situation, we many have energetic cords reaching to that past point in time. Clearing and releasing those cords makes more energy available for the present moment in our lives.

Exercise: Energetic Cord Clearing

When you work with Air for energetic attunement, it is profoundly important to look at the ways in which you are energetically connected to others. Are you running your own energy, or do you need to clear energy between yourself and others? When you have unresolved issues with others (things you haven't forgiven, or memories that you keep reliving), you stay tied to those people, and they to you, through energetic cords. Energetic release work on your old relationships will fully release your ties to the past and make you and your energy fully present in the now. You can work with your intention and go through your past relationships one-by-one, releasing each energetic cord that needs to be released.

In a meditative state, imagine yourself sitting before a campfire at the center of a circle of protective fire. Then, call in any guides or teachers you would like to have as support. Next, call in the person you want to work with (for example, a sister) and tell that person that you are releasing his or her energy from your body. Tell the individual anything else you need to about the relationship -- anything unsaid from the past or anything you feel needs to be cleared. Then ask if there is anything that person would like to say to you. If it is needed and you are ready, do any forgiveness work that needs to be done, and then thank this person for being your teacher. Now scan your body to locate the energetic cords connecting you to this other person. Pull the energetic cords out of your body to release them and seal the release location with love. (Sometimes the cord is deep and has roots like a tree.) Imagine yourself putting the cords into the center campfire so the energy can be transformed. Next call your power back from this other person and breathe deeply to bring your power back into your body.

You can ask to release any vows, agreements, contracts, or karma you have with this person, and breathe until you feel those move out of your body as well. Now thank and release this individual, then thank your guides and teachers on the inner realm for supporting you, and bring your attention back into the room. This exercise provides a potent way to assist in clearing old energies with someone to make more room for clear and clean creational energy in the present.

Also, sometimes things need to be done in the physical realm to continue to shift the energy. A woman who attended a workshop I lead a few years ago was working with her financial situation. While she did energetic clearing with her ex-husband, we realized she still had a checking account that had his name on it years after their divorce. She needed to physically close the account and energetically shift his access to her financial affairs. This made a big difference in her financial flow and abundance. While in meditation, you will want to ask if there is anything for you to physically to do to clear the energetic cords.

Mass Consciousness

Air is the one element we constantly share. As we breathe out and another person breathes in, Air circulates, moving from person to person and place to place. Thus, this element holds group consciousness or the consciousness of the masses. Notice what is being sent out on the airwaves to the masses. Is it love, or fear, or both? We can consciously choose our response. Do we want to align with the energy of the masses and what they hold as true, or choose to focus our own thoughts and energy? Even in times of fear and turmoil we can choose to hold thoughts of peace and love. Each person's thoughts and beliefs add to the collective consciousness, so anytime any one of us comes to greater awareness and clears old emotional baggage or old beliefs, that person adds to the upliftment of mass consciousness.

Meditation and Prayer

In meditation and prayer, we learn how to quiet our mind and receive inner wisdom and guidance. We use prayer to ask for assistance on the inner realm. Meditation provides us with a powerful way to listen and receive guidance. When we pray, it is important to know that our prayers are answered because this feeling sets a vibrational tone. If we pray from an unsure position, we energize our insecurity. We must know that when we hold the frequency of our request it is done.[4]

Music

The Air realm brings one of its most precious gifts in music. It can inspire us, causing our soul to sing and our body to dance. When we feel music in our bodies and notice our response to it, we open our soul to the subtle vibration and variations of creation. Musical rhythms reflect the patterns of the cosmos. Music is the sound of Spirit moving through us, and the music of life sings uniquely through each of us. Dancing to its pulse brings our creations into being.

Peace

Often we struggle with an internal battle of right-brain versus left-brain, head versus heart, being versus doing, masculine versus feminine, or giving versus receiving. Air teaches us that just as inhaling is as vital as exhaling, we need both sides of our brain to think completely.

Different sides of our brain help us perceive things differently. Whole brain thinking is crucial for increasing our mental capacity and our ability to access multidimensional consciousness. The right side of the brain allows us to access creative ideas, intuition, and our psychic gifts while our left-brain helps us focus, compute, analyze, and discern. We need both sides for maximum brain functioning, and we need to cultivate the ability to move between and utilize the different sides of the brain. When we can access the skills they both offer, we can bring our creative ideas fully into form.

As we move into deeper states of whole brain thinking, our ability to access inner peace increases and we begin to think holographically and multidimensionally. In addition, our understanding of the mysteries and relevance of Sacred Geometry expands, thus increasing our level of perception and perspective of the universe. Peace prevails as the dualistic struggles within us are resolved and all parts of ourselves are brought into the whole.

Perspective

Perspective provides a key to understanding how our life functions. Air can teach us how to look both at the larger view and to focus in on the details. From the Air realm, we can see the larger perspective of our life by simply soaring above it and looking down, much as a hawk or eagle would from the sky. We accomplish this by moving our consciousness to the far reaches of the cosmos to gain a cosmic perspective. Air gives us the ability to look at ourselves from the widest possible view and from multiple perspectives. Imagine looking down on any issue at hand from the perspective of the hawk.

This gives us the ability to see how our individual life and life expression affects our family, our community, our state, the nation in which we live, the world, and the universe. None of us lives in a vacuum. Air gives us the ability to look at ourselves from the widest possible view and from multiple perspectives, providing us with the ability to be visionary both in our personal life and in the world.

Exercise: Creating A New Perspective

When we hold old views of the people in our lives, we don't give them room to show up around us authentically and to behave in a manner that differs from our picture of them. Have you ever heard your family talk about you as if you were the same as you were twenty years ago? That makes it difficult to show up to them as who you are now. You may be doing the same with others, thinking you know who they are based on an old perspective. When you allow yourself to release the old pictures of who they were, you might find a big shift in the way you see them now. A shift in perception allows room for everyone to show up in new ways.

Movement offers us a great way to do this release work. Choose some wild dance music, and before you turn on the music, set an intention to break the old pictures you hold of each person in your life so they can show up as who they are now. When you turn on the music and dance, see in your mind's eye a picture frame of that person. Then imagine throwing it to the ground, breaking it, and releasing them from the old frame. Do this until no more images of people appear.

Now, imagine you are sweeping up the pile of broken picture frames to clear the energy in the room where you danced. In the Air realm, things function invisibly and you can't see the effect of the energy you are working with like you can with Earth, Water, or Fire; but you will definitely notice the effects of doing this kind of work in your life. The people around you will surprise you with the new ways they show up in your life.

In a workshop, a woman asked me this question: "I am different now and the people around me keep treating me from their old perspective. How can I change them?" I responded: "Are you still holding the picture that they will treat you the same as they always have?" Realizing she was holding that picture, this woman did release work about how she thought others were going to respond to her, thus making room for the new to emerge. This made a significant difference in her relationships. We also may need to release the pictures and perspectives we have of ourselves.

Soaring

Air offers the ability to take flight, bringing the feeling of soaring and freedom within our lives. Air gives us the wings of freedom. When we have consciously set the tone for our life and are thinking and holding a positive perspective, we feel vibrant, radiant, uplifted, and free. Without enough

Air and the upliftment that Air brings, we can feel stuck as if things in our life have become stale and stagnant. We can breathe life into our world by connecting with Air and some of the vibrational modalities for healing and upliftment that use Air. A good dose of Air infuses life with a sense of the ability to take flight. Deep breathing frees the body. To feel Air's freedom, get out in the fresh air with time to explore. In the mental realm, imagination frees us and helps us soar.

Thoughts

Thoughts possess creative vibration and power. Each thought is like a seed carrying the energy of beingness. It has substance in the realm of creation; it is a "thing." Thoughts play an enormously important role in our co-creations. They tune our inner Water vibrationally, attracting what we draw into our life. Consciously choosing our thoughts helps us to responsibly direct this creational power.

Directing our thought power also includes listening to the wisdom of the other elemental realms when they bring us messages. For example, Water can bring to the surface of our awareness an emotion that needs to be fully felt so it can be cleared, making room for our next creation to come into being. Only by allowing those feelings to be honored and experienced, do we gain all the insight Water brings. If we over-ride our feelings by focusing primarily on our mental realm, dismissing and judging our feelings, we will miss the powerful messages and guidance they carry.

The same holds true of Earth's messages brought to us in the form of our body's wise assistance, or when Fire brings a transformational event into our life. As part of our ability to work with Air as a tool of creation, we must also learn to hold and honor the wisdom of all the elemental realms, as well as our guidance from Spirit. We want to increase our capacity to discern the messages brought from other realms and then to use our thoughts to assist us in understanding what we need. The forces work together and honor one another in this way.

Exercise: Consciously Observing Thoughts

As you increase your ability to observe your thoughts, you will find there are times you have a thought or say something you do not actually want to energize in your life. If you speak or think something that you immediately realize you do not want to manifest, you can say "cancel" or "clear" to erase the creative energy of the undesired words. Also, be sure to state aloud or silently what you do choose to energize. You want to leave on the screen of your mind your desired outcome.

Vibrational Attunement Modalities

A tremendous variety of Air-related tools can uplift our energy. Aromatherapy, essential oils, flower essences, crystals, color, sound, polarity therapy, magnetic therapy, feng shui, and smudging with sage, copal, and incense each assist us in raising energetic frequencies. These modalities help us vibrationally attune our homes, offices, or physical bodies.

Smell travels through the air and is a powerful tool for personal healing and uplifting energy. Working with color and color therapy is a way of using our vision, which is related to Air, to shift our vibration. We can also actively increase our vibration by visually connecting with the beauty of the natural world. Flowers have a very high vibration, so visiting a botanical garden increases the body's vibration, as does work with flower essences. Flowers have a profound effect on our energetic system.

Sound healing uses the vibration of tone and music to deeply influence our energy and vibration. By listening to different types of music, experimenting with crystal and Tibetan bowls, or toning, we can notice how our energy system feels and changes.

Working with crystals provides an effective way to heal the physical body and increase our vibration. They hold an energetic grid that helps us access other levels of awareness as well.

Visionary Abilities

Air governs our ability to envision our life. Here we activate our visionary ability for the larger community, the world, and ourselves. When we create a vision or work with our visionary abilities, we begin creating from our ideas and pictures of what our world can be like. The pictures we hold start drawing energy to them. If we want to bring our highest good into manifested or created form, it is critical that these pictures be of the highest possible outcome. Looking at the big picture helps us create our best possible inner vision.

Exercise: Activating Your Visionary Ability

A few years ago, while I was participating in a sharing circle, a native elder passed around a talking stick that had been in his family for generations. This powerful medicine tool had an eagle head at its top. The minute I touched the stick, I saw through the eagle's eyes as it soared above the earth, and eagle asked me "Do you have the courage to be the visionaries of these times?" This one simple question affected me deeply, because I understood the meaning. Each of us carries the capacity to envision a world where we honor one another and the natural world around us. The eagle was asking me if we each have the courage to be those visionaries.

Sit in meditation and, if it feels appropriate to you, ask Air and eagle energy to activate your visionary ability. Ask if there are ways in which you need to be more courageous in your life or in your vision of life? Ask if there is anything else you need to know. Receive the messages given and journal about it. You may also want to do a visionary collage or art piece.

Dear Air,
thank you for the gifts you bring as we listen
to the whispers of the wind for ways to finely tune
our frequency and our lives. Through your teachings
we find a space of inner receptivity and deep listening
as we develop the soul quality of peace and access the
powers of intention, focus, and vibration.

CHAPTER SIX

Fire

"Everything in the universe has rhythm.

Everything dances."

Maya Angelou

*F*ire

Action Realm

Mystery School Teachings:
Shamanism, tantra, dance, accessing life force, taking action on your own behalf, right use of power.

Developmental Task:
Fully running your life force

Key Word: Dynamic

Soul Quality: Passion

Ecstatic Realm: Energized

Primary Power: Action

Level 2 Power: Shamanic Consciousness

Natural Rhythm Cycle: Day and Night

*F*ire governs the realm of energy and action, where we learn to become dynamic, to claim our personal power, to let our light shine brightly, and to feel enthusiasm for life. Fire also teaches us about the mysteries of transformation, literally how to change forms, to die to an old part of the self, and to be born anew. A volatile realm, often people express their fear of Fire getting out of control. Learning to work with Fire requires focus, and conscious training, and, ultimately, balance.

Fire teaches us to live a dynamic, powerful, and passionate life from our radiant core, our deep inner fire. At the same time, working effectively with Fire requires that we honor in our everyday awareness the sacred teachings, tools, and messages from other elemental realms.

Fire is the element of light: the rays of the sun, the soft glow of candles, the radiance of a roaring fire, and the illumination of our consciousness. Under the influence of Fire, we can shine light on our inner awareness to discover what has previously remained hidden in the darkness of our unconscious. As we shine the light of consciousness within us, we awaken to the process of bringing forth our Radiant Self. Our Radiant Self is the shining, bright, full, whole, knowing, expanded essence-self at the core of each individual. Illumined or Christed beings have fully activated this energy in themselves.

At its core, each spark of Spirit possesses an innate desire to move toward growth and expansion, and an impulse to move toward the full expression of its pure essence. Fire provides both the spark and the fuel for that growth and expression. Individuals, plants, animals, projects, books, businesses, relationships, cities, and countries begin life with the potential for growth, change, and the development of full expression. When people express their expanded, fully-expressive, radiant selves, they are filled with life force, and this energy makes them enlivening and inspiring to be around. They radiate a deep sense of personal power and authority. Such people have completed the inner development necessary to run and work fully with their inner Fire. To remain burning and internally and externally balanced, the powerful force of Fire requires much attention.

Fire Skills and Powers

When working with Fire, we first need to develop the skill of "right use of power." In other words, we need to learn how to use power in an appropriate manner, effectively directing our personal power without using it as power over others. Over the centuries, Fire's ability to overpower has been used frequently to control people through fear. For example, the threats of possibly burning forever in the afterlife or of being burned at the stake have been used to control many people all over the world. It is fascinating that the threat of larger amounts of Fire has provided the tool so often used for controlling Fire itself.

Historically, we have dampened, or controlled, other peoples' Fire by instilling fear in them. When we dampen a person's Fire -- their passion, life force, or sexuality, we control a large part of their personal power. The basis of each person's personal power is formed in their ability to take action on their own behalf, but without imposing their power over others, to create their dreams and visions for their lives, their families, and their communities.

Guns, bombs, and the burning of villages have been used to dominate, as well as to protect. Thus, it becomes clear that how we use Fire provides a critical component in our learning to work with Fire responsibly. Power can be misused by controlling or dominating others, or it can be expressed in balanced and effective ways, such as in the power to take action on our own behalf.

If we want to work closely with Fire, the ability to use power appropriately will serve us well. To increase our consciousness and skills with Fire, we can ask ourselves questions such as: Do we instill fear in others to accomplish our desires? Are others using fear to manipulate us? Can we find ways to use our personal power to effectively empower our life and our life choices? Can we stand in our power and allow others to do the same?

As we work with the elemental forces, we gain wisdom and skill at further accessing our personal power. Having control over our own personal power and life force allows us to take action on our own behalf and to manage our own life most effectively. Our life is propelled forward in the action realm. Learning to take action on our own behalf, as well as in alignment with the greater good, represents Fire's primary power. Action allows us to align with Spirit in our own creations. Spirit needs us as the vehicle for taking action in the world. Our passion serves as the fuel that propels our action in life.

Activation & Exercise: Fire's Power of Action

Preferably, do this exercise standing. If for any reason you cannot stand, your intention will work to activate the power while you are seated. Find a great piece of music that feels good to you for this activation. Before putting on the music, state your intention out loud or silently in your head to activate Fire's power of action. Place your awareness in your body. Then, put on your music and dance to activate, enliven, and embody the power of action. Once complete with the dance, put your awareness into your body, and ask Fire what else you need to know to more fully utilize the power of action in your life. Listen internally for the answer and journal about the response.

After your initial journaling, ask your inner Fire to tell you ten things upon which you need to take action in your life. Do you have a lack of Fire in your life? If so, these items might have been on your mental list for a long time. Have you been procrastinating about taking important actions needed to move you to the next level of development? Perhaps you have an over abundance of Fire. Do you do too much? Do you now need quiet reflection and integration time? As you work with your list, notice how your life force is freed as you begin completing your ten items.

The importance of noticing how we feel about taking action on our own behalf and towards our own goals and dreams cannot be stressed enough. Frustration, anger, or regret, over actions we've not taken robs us of energy. In fact, we may have energy we need to reclaim and free so we can fully reclaim our power. If we have given our personal power away to others, to organizations, or to out-dated belief systems, the time may have come to release and to let go so we can develop.

To release energy draining our personal power, we must first notice if we have anger, regret, or frustration tied up with any old memories. Only when we delve into the situation that created those memories or the memories themselves, and uncover the feelings associated with them, can we release the personal power connected to that situation. We also want to notice if we believe it was someone else's fault the situation happened. As adults, we can claim responsibility for the situation by simply noticing how we allowed it; then, we can fully reclaim our personal power. If we were children when the situation occurred, we might have to work through deep layers of emotion before we can learn the lessons our experiences have to teach us.

When conducting clearing work, memories function the same as current situations. Ask yourself questions, such as: What could I have done that would have produced a different result? How can I take better care of myself next time? Does the other person have my personal power? If you have relinquished your power, then you can mentally call your personal power back and claim it for yourself again. Then, check to see if you are angry with yourself and acknowledge any ways in which you might feel angry at yourself for the situation. After that, look at the places where you didn't take the necessary action, didn't express what needed to be said, or acted in ways you regret. At this point, you can forgive yourself and others as necessary to reclaim your personal power and live fully in the present.

The development of shamanic consciousness represents Fire's level two power. The shaman of an indigenous tribe served as the medicine man or woman, the person the people went to for healing on the physical, emotional, and spiritual levels. A shamanic healer uses both outer world and inner world tools and can access information beyond ordinary awareness. In fact, well-developed shamans have the ability to see with their outer eyes and their inner eyes, which means they can see in the light and in the dark. Every element and archetype has ways in which it develops and works with the unseen inner realm -- the darkness (as in the night energies), things growing in the womb, the subconscious or unconscious, and the places previously hidden in the psyche.

Shamans see what is visible in the light of day -- in our ordinary awareness -- and what is invisible and in other realms that requires extraordinary perception. In the latter, they discover what is hidden and ready to come to the light of understanding. Shamans have developed within themselves the ability to work with the energies of healing, nature, and unseen realms. They access wisdom through non-ordinary means, such as by taking inward journeys to retrieve needed information. An effective shaman can travel into many other realms of consciousness to bring back what is required for healing.

When we develop shamanic consciousness for ourselves, we enliven our ability to see into what is hidden in our own lives. This allows us to see what needs to be brought into the light so we can increase our awareness and our wholeness. The activation of shamanic consciousness offers us a potent skill that we can use for connecting deeply to the sacred in all life.

Those who have integrated all the elements and who can work with both the yin and yang energies can use Fire's powerful tools. One who is ready for the activation of shamanic consciousness will draw a mentor to them or will access the information for this activation through their own inner work.

Sometimes this training comes to us through an inner initiation called "the dark night of the soul."[1] We experience this as a period of life when we feel left alone in the dark to deal with all our inner shadows. It can be brought on by external events, such as a divorce, the death of a loved one, a financial disaster, a medical crisis, the loss of a job, turning a certain age, or from several things happening all at once. Or this initiation can come simply from a feeling of disquiet and frustration about life in general. No matter how it arrives, it takes us to the deepest places in our inner awareness to see what is hidden there. In our dark night, we experience our deepest fears and all the parts of ourselves that have been unloved, rejected, or projected on to others.

When we find ourselves in the dark night of the soul, we possess little energy for the outside world. All our attention turns towards being with ourselves inwardly. In a culture that puts so much focus on outer-world achievement and the meeting of goals, it can be challenging to find the support we need to stay on our inner journey. Well-meaning friends and colleagues may attempt to cheer us up, help us out of our depression or grief, or move us into outward pursuits. Support for those in a dark night of the soul, however, looks quite different. They need support to fully feel all their emotions, look at their shadow, and stay with the process until it is complete. This natural cycle in the soul's evolution brings us a profound level of inner depth and power, if we can travel through the dark inner terrain until we reach the other side and the light of day naturally enters.

Upon emerging from this initiation, we will find ourselves more integrated and possessing a deeper capacity for compassion and soul work. The darkness we travel through holds the seeds of the next layer we must bring forth or birth into the outer world. We don't know this or have access to this information while we are in the darkness, because we only can see glimpses of the potential. Once we have completed the initiation, however, we receive all the gifts of the journey -- including a vision of the future we will create. A dark night of the soul initiation begins the development of shamanic consciousness -- and expands our ability to see in the dark inner realms. Once we have this skill, we can fully bring the resources we need to the light of day.

Fire's Developmental Task

As part of inner Fire development we must learn how to fully and appropriately allow our life force energy to flow through our bodies. Most of us were born with an exuberant amount of life force, the vital essence that propels us forward. In our early childhood, we usually find ourselves full of vibrant life force energy, but as we become acculturated that energy frequently gets controlled and muted.

Unless we consciously keep our life force activated and flowing as we go through life, we may decrease the amount of life force flowing through our body. Our culture often trains us early on to close down our Fire by teaching us to sit still, be quiet, and not get too excited, happy, sexual, or passionate. Yet our life force provides us with the energy and power to energize our dreams. When we find ways to fully allow our life force energy to run through our bodies and to influence our lives, it changes our lives in potent ways. Our body becomes enlivened, our Radiant Self begins to emerge, and we have the energy needed to take action toward manifesting our creations.

Fear and the suppression of anger block our life force. When we feel fear, it puts our system into survival mode instead of into the thriving mode that aids co-creation. When we hold back our anger, we hold back much of our power and our life force. We don't need to act out our anger in unhealthy ways, but we do need to find healthy and effective ways to feel and release it. When we learn to deal with our anger effectively, it releases a clear flow of life force.

Because fear is used so often to control Fire, this emotion may be blocking our personal power and our life force. We may have a fear of shining too brightly, being fully seen, taking action, being fully in our power, or taking the next step in our development. Having the courage to move through our fears takes enormous conviction on our part. It also takes practice. We must learn to trust that we can and do know how to take the steps necessary to achieve our dreams. Practice and trust develop one step at a time.

As we move through our fear, we may discover pockets of emotional suppression. In our culture, as in most cultures, we have unacceptable and acceptable emotional norms. Both men and women have culturally-defined limits to their expression of emotion. Until recently, it wasn't acceptable for men and boys of a certain age to cry, so they learned to suppress their sadness or pain. This often led to the repression of their most tender feelings and an over-development of anger and aggression. As men unblock their sadness and learn to appropriately express their pain, they will find it releases their highest personal power, and it can fuel the actions they need to take.

Women, on the other hand, often have been taught to suppress their anger. Nice girls and women simply were not supposed to get angry. Instead of feeling their anger, they frequently would cry in a situation that would perhaps be better handled by allowing themselves to fully feel and express their anger and heed its message. Women who only release their emotions through tears often dampen their personal power in the process. As women unblock and appropriately express their anger, they will find it releases their personal power, to fuel the actions they need to take.

With few culturally-acceptable ways to work with Fire, we instead learn ways to tamp it down through the over use of alcohol, drugs, sex, money, work and anything else that mutes our powerful life force. In our attempt to learn to work with Fire, we also may burn ourselves out or play too close to the edge. We need to learn, or relearn, how to work with Fire productively.

An enormous amount of our inner Fire development comes from

learning how to reclaim our life force, to allow it to fully run through our bodies, and to live life with it pulsing through our veins. Movement serves as one of the most important enliveners of life force. Fire constantly moves. Watch a candle and notice that even a small flame is in motion all the time. For us to increase the Fire energy in our lives, we need to get our bodies in motion. The interesting thing about Fire is that sometimes you have to coax it to burn more by blowing Air on it so it will get stronger. In our lives, we increase our life force by applying the Air tools of intention and focus to get ourselves out of our chair and up and moving.

Activation: Life Force

Put on your favorite piece of music, and ask Fire to activate your life force. Now dance, and let your life force pulsate through your body. When you are finished, ask your life force for any messages it has for you. Ask if there are ways you need to run it more fully through your body. Listen internally for the answer to your question, and then record the answer in your journal.

Natural Rhythm Cycle: Day and Night

Fire, the fuel that drives us to action, activates our passions and desires, which, in turn, compel us to move forward with our lives. Fire serves as the vital spark that ignites movement. Fire urges the seeds of all sorts to spring to life -- those in the ground and warmed by the sun, or those in the human body fueled by the Fire of sexual passion. No matter the situation, Fire acts as the initiator of growth, the activator of life force.

Dancer & Musical Note:
The day's **24** hours can be divided into several musical rhythms, one of which is called **3/8**. Those **3** divisions of **8** divides our day into **8** hours of sleep, **8** hours of work/activity, and **8** hours of self-care including rest, eating, exercise, personal hygiene, and social connections.

Just as seeds placed in the soil need the warmth of the sun to heat the soil for germination, the seeds of our desires need Fire, the vibrant passionate life energy, to activate energy for their creation. Our inner Fire activates the seeds of our desires. Our inner Fire, our spark of passion, activates our creations. When we feel "fired up" about something, we can accomplish tremendous feats with little effort on our part, because Fire provides powerful fuel for our efforts.

12:00 *Midnight*

6:00 PM

6:00 AM

12:00 *Noon*

As with any fuel, we want to use the right amount at the right time. When working with Fire, we need to achieve balance. From cooking to relationships or work, too much Fire can too quickly burn the energy of whatever we get involved in or choose to create, causing us or it to burn out. Yet, Fire does the cooking, generates the passion, inspires our desires, and provides the necessary fuel. To work most effectively with Fire, we need the stability of the other elements to help us achieve the correct balance. In addition, we need to carefully tend our Fire.

To effectively ignite our inner Fire, we need earthen bodies strong enough to burn the amount of Fire energy we access. To use our Fire appropriately, we need balanced emotions, and to guide our Fire effectively we need to use our Air wisdom. Additionally, we need our actions to be in alignment with our Spirit-directed desires. The balanced and unified work of all the elements and Spirit brings us the greatest capacity to turn up our Fire when needed.

Through the daily movement of the sun, Fire shares guidance with us about effective balance. The sun lights up the day, bringing the energy for action and growth. Then, it shows us how to cool the heat of action by resting and turning within each evening. The partial light of the moon and the darkness that night brings feels very different than the bright fullness of daytime sunlight. Darkness provides us with the opportunity for quiet nurturance, to balance the intense activity of the day. By honoring the power of rest, nurturance, and turning within, we keep our personal Fire realm in harmony and balance.

Power times are built into each rhythmic cycle. For instance, the yearly cycle has its powerful times of the solstices, equinoxes, and cross quarter days. The moon has the potency of the dark, new, and full moons. Fire's cycle of day and night offers effective times for extra creational juice - dawn and dusk. At these two times of day, the light and dark are changing places, yet they remain together in our awareness. This makes both of them more accessible and unites them in support of our creations.

Remember how the energies originally unfolded: First, they divided into two -- yin/yang, and masculine/feminine. The division continued to create the four elements and directions, then into the eight points of the Wheel of the Year and the moon cycle, then the 12 astrological gates of awareness. At this stage, the division continues into the 24 hours of the day. This mathematical progression expresses similarly to many of the time signatures in music and shows us the tremendous organization of the rhythms of the universe. The more we align our personal energy flow to these organizing principles, the greater becomes our ability to harmonize with the natural flowing grace of life.

Additional Fire Mystery School Teachings

Altered States

Fire shows us how to transform our ordinary awareness into an extra-ordinary state of consciousness. In fact, we need only stare long enough into a fire to travel deeper into our consciousness and experience new awareness. In addition, Fire teaches us ways to increase our perception through deep trance-like states, achieved with use of a wide variety of methods. When we access these states, we directly connect with the Divine, and need no intermediary to make the connection on our behalf. We make the direct link, with Fire bringing us back home to our personal power. This non-ordinary awareness brings us deep gifts of inner knowing.

Indigenous and native people around the world have accessed altered states of consciousness and journeyed in other worlds and realms with Fire path tools. Through study and work with modern shamans, we can learn techniques to awaken these facets of our consciousness. Ceremony, trance dance, breath work, journey work, mask-making, drumming, and sacred sexuality represent just a few methods that teach us to activate our life force in safe settings and to access our inner world, thus bringing us profound revelations and deep insights.

Used in a ritual environment, consciousness altering tools, such as firewater and plant teachers, take people into altered levels of awareness within a sacred context. These potent Fire tools used outside a sacred context also can thrust people into a state of madness, dependence, and abuse. Working in this realm requires a fine edge of honor and balance and experienced expert guidance.

In spiritual traditions, a person would achieve a high degree of mastery with the other elements before working with altered states of consciousness. Prior to entering an altered state, one must have developed emotional maturity, know how to hold a clear sacred container, and keep their mental realm strong. Fire teaches people to move beyond their ordinary reality. Bridging the seen and unseen worlds, they enter the world of the shaman, the medicine man or woman.

Exercise: Creating With Fire

Set up a dance journey for yourself of four to six pieces of rhythmic musical pieces that contain no words. When the music begins, set your intention that you want to connect with your Radiant Self. Then travel on the music's rhythm to connect with your Radiant Self. As you do, ask for any guidance that it might have for you. Once complete with your journey, make a shamanic mask of your Radiant Self. Then, put on your mask and stand in front of the mirror. Ask your Radiant Self to tell you about itself -- you. Journal about any insights you gain. This exercise provides a wonderful way to enter into an altered state, bridging the inner and outer worlds and working with your creative Fire energy.

Energized

Juiced by our inner firepower, we become vibrantly alive and an abundance of life force energy runs through our bodies. When we follow our passion and find ways to enliven ourselves, we energetically engage life and become energized. We express life in a dynamic and inspired manner. Some people possess a naturally dynamic nature that gets the energy in and around them in motion. Others have to be more conscious about raising their heat and getting their energy moving. Rhythm, dance, sexuality -- anything that builds the feeling of ecstatic union between body, soul, and Spirit -- works as an energizer. We need to be energized to fuel our co-creations.

Illumination

Under the influence of Fire, we shine light on our inner awareness to discover what has previously remained hidden. We awaken to deeper inner knowing, wisdom, and guidance as the light shines within our consciousness. When we need to see something, we look to the element of Fire for assistance.

 **Exercise: Illumination**
While either sitting in meditation or dancing to music with a rhythmic beat, ask Fire to illuminate your understanding of something about which you need awareness. Then journal about Fire's response, and allow yourself to take action on the wisdom given.

Letting Go

Stepping into the new phase of anything requires letting go of the old phase and of our familiar ways of functioning in that phase. Like the snake shedding its skin, we need to release what we no longer need so we have room to grow and to move forward into the next level of being. Letting go feels scary, however, which explains why we often want to know with certainty what is coming next and how it is going to fully play out before we let go of what is known. Yet the transformational process of change rarely works that way. Often after burning the old, we experience a period of not knowing before the new is born from the ashes. Honoring the transformational phase of a process requires trust and letting go is just the first stage.

Move

Existing in the action realm, Fire's main activity involves movement. Fire teaches us to move our energy, move our body, move our life forward, and move out of situations that don't serve us.

Dance provides an exceptional tool for igniting our life force, and in all its forms, it helps keep our life force open and flowing. In general, dance and movement serve as crucial Fire tools. When a level of social change occurs, dance and music generally can be found at the forefront of that change. In some cultures, people have felt fear around certain types of dance when they perceived it as too radical, different or promiscuous. For instance, this happened when the dances performed to waltz, jazz, and rock and roll music first were introduced. In some cultures, the regulation of dance has been used as a means to control, because when people don't move or move in very limited ways their thinking, as well as their life force and power, becomes restricted.

If we want to free our thinking, increase our creativity, or free a block in our life, we literally need to move in new ways. Finding new movements shifts our energy. For this reason, dance has been used to free overly-tight constraints around the physical body, or the way people perceive the world, and to bring in new levels of perception.

Dance gives us a powerful tool for moving deep issues and energies as well. It tremendously enlivens life force. Dancing to strongly percussive music, with little or no words, serves this purpose very effectively. Shamans have used the ancient tools of ritual drumming and dance for transforming energy, spiritual journeying, and achieving trance states. The rhythmic music and dance moves participants into a trance state, allowing them access to inner realms and awareness not found in their ordinary reality. This type of dance can be used for increasing personal expression, opening to creative insight, and accessing deep levels of soul transformation.

Sensuality

When we are fully present in our body and connected to our life force, we connect to our sensuality. This brings the pleasure of the physical body into harmony with the energy of Spirit. Sensuality brings richness to everything we touch, from our clothes, to our food, to our loved ones, to all of the other things we experience in our daily lives.

Sexual Energy

Our sexuality powers our creative energy. It provides us with the ability to physically create new life, and we can use that same power to create a new life for ourselves. Imagine the possibilities presented to us if we use that energy fully. What could or would we create if we realized the depth and true power of our creative capabilities? However, most people do not access and use that creative power to its fullest extent. When that energy gets suppressed in our bodies we become bored, sad, depressed and feel lifeless.

Culturally, we have been bombarded with mixed messages about this powerfully-creative force, and as a result, we have been disconnected from its sacred power. When sexuality is taken out of the context of sacredness, it often becomes degrading to those participating. Then, people find themselves treated as objects instead honored as beautiful expressions of the Divine.

Tantra is a teaching and path of sacred sexuality. In Tantra, a couple in union acknowledges the sacred in each other, which takes both of them into a deeper connection with Spirit. Their union with each other and with Spirit increases their inner radiance, creating an external glow and new internal awareness. Sacred sexuality channels passion into an increased consciousness for the individuals who practice its path, as well as for the collective transformation of the planet.

Transformation

Transformation occurs when something changes shape or form. To say something "changed form" implies that a form existed previously that could go through a process of release and transformation. Every elemental force has a way that it destroys. Earthquakes, floods, tornadoes, fires, and other natural disasters bring about the destruction that so often changes the form and shape of lives. Some form of destruction usually precedes creation as the old form is released to make way for the new. Destruction and death signify normal parts of the cycle of life and birth in the natural world of form.

Sometimes we want something new in our lives, yet we do not want to release what is familiar, easy, and safe. With any transformational process, we must learn to let go of what we currently have and the stage in which we currently exist if we want in to move to the next level. Fire initiates growth and growth brings with it the need to let go of our old ways of life. Fire releases the previous form by reducing it to ashes. The ash becomes the soil for new growth. Fire takes the form down to the basest level -- destruction -- before the rebuilding process can begin.

The challenge with letting go lies in the fact that it requires that we step into the unknown. The unknown can seem to us be a frightening or uncomfortable place. In order to grow, we are required to move beyond our personal comfort zone and into the new. This is a frightening prospect for some of us and involves learning to feel comfortable with some degree of risk -- or at least being willing to feel uncomfortable until we acclimate to living with the risk.

In the transformational process, completely releasing and letting go requires letting go of all the old ways we've defined ourselves and the world around us. Our habitual ways of perceiving ourselves run deep in our psyche, yet we must release these perceptions if we are to move into our fully radiant selves. To allow ourselves to become empowered and radiant beings full of life force, we must leave behind any beliefs that we are less than others, or limited in our capabilities, and we must instead embrace our powerful radiance.

Fire provides the energy for the transformation of substances. It warms the soil for the seed to sprout and provides the heat for the grain to grow. Once the grain is harvested, we grind it into flour and then further transform it into dough that rises as it is prepared to bake. Fire provides the heat to bake the bread, turning it into the substance we consume as food. Once inside the body Fire provides the digestive heat to transform the bread into fuel.[2]

When we apply the heat of Fire to the raw ingredients for cooking, Fire transforms it into something delicious to eat that nourishes us. Applied to our life, Fire forges the substance of our being, much as steel is fashioned into a sword with the power of the flame. However, it takes a great deal of trust to allow the transformative power of Fire to take place.

Exercise: Exploring Transformation

Over the years, I have worked with many people who were in a process of transformation and who wanted to know clearly what they were transforming into before they were willing to let go of their current stage. The process simply doesn't work that way; we have to trust the process and allow it to happen. Often people think they have done something "wrong" and that all the things leaving or changing in their lives represent some sort of "punishment." At certain points of our lives, as transformation takes place things naturally fall away so we can fully awaken to our newly-expanded self. Many of us grow up expecting our adults lives to stay stable -- basically the same. Understandably, we may have little trust and much fear or disbelief in the transformational process, and we need practice and support to allow our changes to occur gracefully.

To explore transformation, sit in a quiet spot near a fire or in the sun and ask Fire what is transforming in your life right now. Then, journal about the response you receive. Ask Fire what you need to let go of to allow the transformation to occur. Are there any limitations you need to release? If there are, make a list on a piece of paper that you can burn. When you've completed the list, burn the paper with the intention that the issues be released in the flames. Consider what you want to replace those limitations with in your consciousness. Make a list of what you want to hold in your awareness during your transformation. Now go for a walk or dance to activate your grace-filled transformation.

Warmth

The soft glow of the candle, the gently-burning fire, warm cookies from the oven, and a cup of hot tea exemplify the serene ways Fire supports our lives. Their muted Fire provides nurturing warmth for the soul as well as for the body. Fire's warmth helps us find peaceful ways in which to balance our lives and to nurture our inner well-being.

Exercise Exploring Warmth

Find a comfortable special spot to sit with Fire near by. You can sit next to a collection of candles or a cozy fire or out in the warm sunshine. Bring something warm to eat or drink, and your journal. Soak up the warmth of the environment and relish the food or drink. Then, ask Fire what it wants to share with you about receiving its warmth. Ask how you need to work with warmth in your life. Journal about the response you receive.

Will

Fire teaches us about the power of our will applied to our actions. Determination, energy, and a fixed purpose help us move forward in alignment with our desires, and stay on a focused course. When using Fire, we must do so in a balanced manner. Misaligned or overused will can prove harmful or keep us stuck in a situation we are ready to move past. Learning the right use of will and the right time to use it, and doing so in alignment with the Divine, provides a core Fire path teaching.

Fire, you are a wonderful teacher.
You help us learn to walk in balance, honoring the sacred
in light and in the darkness, in the outer and the inner realms.
Thank you for teaching us ways to live a dynamic,
powerful, and passionate life from our radiant core.
We lovingly express our gratitude for your spark of life
and for being the fuel for our growth.

Blessed be.

CHAPTER SEVEN

Spirit

"Learning to walk sets you free.

Learning to dance gives you the greatest

freedom of all: to express with your whole self,

the person you are."

Melissa Hayden

Our apology for the error -
The first three paragraphs on page 189 should read as follows:

*A*t the core of all creation lies Spirit, the essence energy of Source. This rich substance flows through and connects Earth, Water, Air, and Fire, and then moves out into all of creation. Spirit expresses as the creational glue that moves through the elements to hold our world in form in both the outer realm and the inner realm. It is the unseen ingredient necessary when the elements work together in any creation. Spirit moves and breathes in all life. We can feel the substance of Spirit, the Source of all that is, when we sit quietly in nature or reflect on our inner nature. In silence or the quiet of nature, we can notice how Spirit resides at the center of every living thing, providing its core essence. We can feel this in both our own individual nature -- our unique Spirit -- and in our connection to all life.

With Spirit as our guide and teacher, we discover that we are human and Divine, active and receptive, yin and yang, individual and connected. We develop our capacity to hold these opposites in our consciousness simultaneously and to understand that our awareness moves between them at different times.

Spirit provides our connection to the Divine, to God/Goddess, and to the essence of all life. With Spirit at our core, we possess a direct connection to the Divine, and that knowing connects us to our own personal divinity. As expressions of Spirit in human form, we are also each a Divine being. Our awareness of our divinity raises our inner vibration and our connection to life.

Spirit continuously reminds us that imperfection simply exists as part of the creative process. Flaws sometimes find their way in after the hundredth correct proof at the eleventh hour, revealing themselves only after arriving from the printer. Imperfections develop character, like the knots found on trees, and remind us to keep creating anyway. Our apology for this error provided us with an opportunity to gift you with something extra. Please log on to www.naturalrhythms.org to download a free full color rendition of the Natural Rhythms Sacred Timings.
-Lisa Michaels

Spirit

Spiritual Realm

Mystery School Teachings:
Expression of the spark of Spirit you are,
Conscious Creation of your own life,
Connection to God/Goddess.

Developmental Task:
Bringing your essence forth

Key Word: Essence

Soul Quality: Compassion

Ecstatic Realm: Divine Union

Primary Power: Choice

Level 2 Power: Co-creation

Natural Rhythm Cycle: Yin/Yang

At the core of all creation lies Spirit, the es... rich substance flows through and connects Eart... then moves out into all of creation. Spirit expresse... moves through the elements to hold our world in f... and the inner realm. It is the unseen ingredient n... work together in any creation.

Spirit moves and breathes in all life. We can... the Source of all that is, when we sit quietly in n... nature. In silence or the quiet of nature, we can... the center of every living thing, providing its core... both our own individual nature -- our unique Spi... to all life.

With Spirit as our guide and teacher, we disc... Divine, active and receptive, yin and yang, individu... our capacity to hold these opposites in our consci... to understand that our awareness moves between...

Spirit provides our connection to the Divine, ... essence of all life. With Spirit at our core, we possess a direct connection to the Divine, and that knowing connects us to our own personal divinity. As expressions of Spirit in human form, we are also each a Divine being. Our awareness of our divinity raises our inner vibration and our connection to life.

We simultaneously develop as individual aspects of Spirit and as fundamental components of the collective consciousness. Our individuation in the physical realm is possible only because of our physical vehicle -- our body. Our body provides the container for Spirit in matter. In many traditions, the Spirit of our individuated self, contained in the physical matter of our body, is called "the Soul." Our Spirit connects us to our Divine essence, while our Soul connects us to our human physical body. As we learn to align our co-creations with our direct Divine connection, in our bodily human form, we become a bridge for Spirit coming into the world of matter and form.

Spirit expresses through each of us as unique and individual beings. Our inner connection to Spirit guides us throughout life to bring our own essence into full expression in the world. We have personal responsibility for responding to the call of Spirit through us and for our Spirit's expression in the world. As Spirit in form, we are also responsible for our own connection to Source energy. We work with Spirit. Spirit does not work alone, nor do we work alone, the two create together. As half of that equation, it is our responsibility to heed the call of Spirit.

Spirit gives us the gift of choice. We have the power to choose our perceptions, how we interact with our feelings, others, the earthly realm, and what actions we are going to take at any point. Then, at any time, we have the power to choose something different. The more conscious we are of our choices and of the intentions behind them, the more our life becomes a direct reflection of that awareness.

Spirit Skills and Powers

We are all co-creators in training, learning from Spirit and the elements how to apply their energies in the conscious creation of our lives. To be able to fully explore our skills, we are given free will -- the power to choose. This sounds like such a simple power, yet it is profound. Choice directs the powers of co-creation. Each time we choose something -- what we will eat, wear, think, do, not do, express, feel, create, or where we will live, work, and play -- we design and define ourselves and our lives. This power of choice gives us the ability to co-create our lives and then change them when appropriate.

As sparks of the Divine living in the Earth realm, we express free will through our choices. Free will means that we direct the forces at our disposal. Even in circumstances when our choices seem very limited, we still have the ability to choose our response to the situation.

Because we have free will and the power of choice we guide the energies of our life through our direction. Additional energetic assistance, available to us on the unseen realms, can not and does not move on our behalf unless we invite and direct them to assist us through our free will. Each of us must call on our guides, teachers, angels, elementals and Spiritual support when we choose to have it available.

Therefore in order to fully access our abilities as co-creators, we need to consciously connect to the Divine. The Divine lives in us all the time, because it provides our core essence. We are part of Spirit, since the Divine makes up all of life. Yet, to make a conscious direct link to the Divine current flowing through us, we need to ask for that connection. Our request can be something simple like, "I ask to be connected to the Divine within." This awakens and directs the energy within so it becomes available for us to draw on mindfully. Once we activate Divinity within, we can use our gift of choice more easily for humanity's and our own personal highest co-creational good. Choice provides the power of Spirit, which works directly with our power of co-creation.[1]

Activation: Spirit's Power of Choice

Preferably, do this exercise standing. If for any reason you cannot stand, your intention will work to activate the power even while you are seated. Find a great piece of music, preferably with no words, that feels Divine to you. Either aloud or silently, ask to connect to the Divine within. Before playing the music, to activate Spirit's power of choice, state your intention out loud or in your head. Place your awareness in your body. Then, put on your music and dance to activate, enliven, and embody your intention. Once complete with the dance, connect with Spirit and the power of choice, and ask if you need to know more to use choice consciously in your life. Listen internally for an answer, and journal about the response you receive.

Spirit is creation energy. When we align with Spirit to manifest or to create, we work in co-creative union with All That Is. Alignment with Spirit moves energy into form in amazing ways, and accessing this energy aligns us with the power of all creation and with the forces of the universe.

The energy of creation and manifestation work hand in hand in varying degrees depending upon our level of personal development. An organic process, creation works in the realm of magic, or the unknown, while manifestation happens in more hu-man-made and clearly defined steps. Children or trees grow organically. Forcing their growth externally in some manner would be unnatural. Growth that occurs naturally comes from the energy of creation.

The difference between manifestation and co-creation can be likened to the difference between two types of ground covers -- pavement and grass. If we want pavement, we call a paving company. The paving company comes, mixes the ingredients, pours the material out, rolls over it with heavy machinery, and we end up with a paved ground cover. We can watch this process, and, if we knew how, and had the materials and the machinery, we even could perform every part of this process ourselves. So, "man," or human provides a key part of man-ifestation.

However, if we want grass, we (or a hired landscaper) prepare the soil, spread the grass seed, water the seed, allow the elements (Earth, Water, Air, and Fire) to combine, and wait for the miracle of life to spring forth. We know we stand a good chance of having grass if we find the best type of seed to buy for our growing environment, the soil is good, and the seed receives enough water, sun, and air movement. However, in this process no guarantee exists that the seed will sprout, and we will end up with grass. That is part of the mystery of creation. A mysterious essence must mix with living substances when creation occurs -- the rich substance of Spirit. Humans assist in creation by preparing the soil, planting the seed, and providing water, and fertilizer. That serves as our part of the co-creation. Spirit's part comes in adding the organic aliveness that brings the rest of the creation forth.

With creation, we always find an element of mystery. For example, a couple trying to conceive a baby never knows which egg and sperm will unite to create a child, or if they even have the energy between them to create another human life. Creation is magical, not logical or practical or predictable.

Yet, creation produces inexplicable and extraordinary results. When we possess desires larger than our ability to manifest them, we may need to call on the power of creation. In other words, when we can find no way to achieve our desire by taking known steps to produce it, we must call on Spirit's power of creation instead of or along with our own power of manifestation. As in the example of conceiving a child, while we know the ingredients to mix for a child, the mystery of its conception, as well as its full healthy development, lies partially out of our hands. Yet, we participate with Spirit to bring this new life into form.

A creation grows mostly in the dark, out of sight, under ground, in a womb, or in our inner consciousness rather than out in the light of day. And we have little control over that process. When a child is *in utero* and then birthed in our world, we know we must surrender to the process, even though we might find it difficult to do so. More often than not, we can't see the growth occurring, and our influence over the outcome is limited. When that same creation process takes place in our lives, we also may have trouble surrendering to the process of waiting for our creation to emerge fully formed.

When we choose to co-create something, we state our intention and make a request to Spirit to bring what we desire into form. We can bring the elements into a unified field -- our part in the co-creation -- and then we must surrender to Spirit's timing of the unfoldment. Just as the pregnant parents must wait, not knowing where or when the contractions and the birthing process will begin, we must wait to see when our creation will begin to take physical form in our lives. Co-creations are unfolding mysteries.

Spirit teaches us how to put the elements into a unified field of awareness and to bring forth our essence for co-creation. We are taught about the magic that happens when we bring forth our desires and then prepare the fertile Earth of our life, by mixing it with our clear flowing emotional Water, the sweet Air of our aligned belief systems, and Fire's power of our actions. When we are able to bring the elements together in this manner, we can open to allow Spirit to begin its magic.

Exercise: Holding a Unified Field

To learn to hold a unified field, review each element's primary power and realm, and then activate their capacity to work together.

Spirit: Ask to connect to the Divine within, your Spirit power of choice, and your essence. Call on your desire to learn to hold an elemental unified field for co-creation.

Air: Connect to your mental realm and your Air power of intention. Ask them to hold an elemental unified field for co-creation.

Water: Connect to your emotional feeling realm and your Water power of love. Ask them to hold an elemental unified field for co-creation.

Fire: Connect to your energetic realm and your Fire power of action. Ask them to hold an elemental unified field for co-creation.

Earth: Connect to your body and the physical realm and your Earth power to stand on your own. Ask them to hold an elemental unified field for co-creation.

Now activate and anchor the unified field in the physical realm through dance, and by putting it in writing, and/or by creating an artistic expression.

Activation: Unified Field

Do this activation only after you have activated the primary power for Earth, Water, Air, Fire, and Spirit. Preferably, do this exercise standing. If for any reason you cannot stand, your intention will work to activate your unified field even while you are seated. Find a great piece of music, preferably with no words, that feels connected to the elements to you. Either aloud or silently, ask to align with all the elements and Spirit and to activate your unified field. Before playing the music, to activate your unified field, state your intention out loud or in your head. Place your awareness in your body. Then, put on your music and dance to activate, enliven, and embody your intention. Once complete with the dance, connect with your unified field, and ask what you need to know to work effectively with it. Listen internally for an answer, and journal about the response you receive.

As we practice holding our unified field to complete the process of bringing our creations fully into form, we may find that we need to fine-tune our ability to work with one or more of the elements. Some people may need to work with Air, increasing their ability to hold a mental picture of what they desire, while others may need to work with Fire to increase their ability to take action. As they work with Fire, they might discover that they are not taking action because of an emotional issue; thus, they need to work with Water. Perhaps, they have a mental belief system that needs updating, and they need to work with Air.

As we work with the elements, we increase our ability to internally follow the clues that indicate where we need to adjust our energy. At certain times, however, we may need a spiritual guide or a teacher, a therapist, counselor, or coach to help us discover the clues being brought to our consciousness. As we work closely with the elements to consciously bring forth our Spirit-filled desires, we will gain practice and skill at seeing any aspect of our creations that may need adjusting.

Let's look at some things we may encounter as we work with the elements and increase our ability both to consciously manifest and to co-create with them. As Spirit calls upon us to express our essence fully in the world, the elements can assist us in the process of creating that reality in our life. For example, perhaps our Spirit has been calling for us to write a book, paint a picture, or develop a new computer program. We need to understand how to work with the elements to bring those creations into form.

Our essence, the pulsation of Spirit through us, brings us our desires. Each of us has unique expression, and, therefore, unique desires. The simple act of listening to our individual desires takes courage, and often bringing the desire into being takes us to our next level of personal growth and development. We need to learn to listen to what our inner voice says about our desires and not just to the calling of the outer world. Sometimes the outer world tells us what we are supposed to desire, but our inner promptings differ from those.

No matter what our particular desire, it will build and grow until we fully recognize our urge to bring it forth. We may begin to wonder how to get our desire into form. Air and the mental realm bring us ideas to sort and sift through. Then we decide which idea or ideas are most worthy of the essence energy required to bring that idea into form.

Often, even simultaneously, we have feelings about our idea and a knowing about what actions need to be taken to bring the desire into earthly form. We become the bridge between our ideas from Spirit and their ability to come into form. We must take the steps necessary to actually write a book and get it bound into earthly form, to paint the picture or to design that computer program. When we receive an essence-driven desire, we get a mental idea of what the desire looks like. Then, we can set our intention for it to come into being and begin focusing our energy upon it. Emotionally, we need to allow ourselves to trust that creation is unfolding and that we will be supported in the process of its development. In our feeling realm we want to hold the knowing of its completion. In addition, we must take the practical action steps required to get the desire into solid, earthly form. Spirit then provides the substance and the synchronicities for the desire to come into being.

These essential steps put the elements into a unified field. There Earth, Water, Air, Fire, and Spirit work in unity and our bodies, feelings, thoughts, actions, and Spirit expressions are aligned energetically. In this unified field of awareness the seeds of creation spring forth from within us.

This process requires us to understand a few additional issues that might arise as we work with it. For instance, sometimes we find that we don't trust our desire. It may be helpful to remember that Spirit uses our desires to push us to grow and to develop, often to reach beyond our current edges of development.

Any true desire we possess has bubbled up within us directly from Spirit. It is our unique desire, and we have the capacity to bring it into being. To know if our desire comes from Spirit, we can check a couple of things. First, we can answer the following questions: Does our desire come from inside us, or is it externally motivated? Do we feel like we need to do something or have something because others do or because we sincerely feel the internal desire? Second, we can discern if our desire contributes to the greater good of the whole. If we feel the desire is internally motivated and contributes to the greater good of the whole, we can trust that it comes from Spirit and will lead us toward growth. The key issue revolves around trusting Spirit and trusting our desires.

We sometimes find ourselves amazed that essence desires are often large. Spirit sends us big desires and big ideas. Frequently, we receive those desires and ideas in a state of development where we see ourselves as much smaller than the desire. We may think, "No not me! I can't do anything like that. Who am I to bring that in or do that?"

Fortunately, Spirit also brings us the power of choice. Having the ability to choose gives us a tremendous power. It enables us to decide where we want to put our energy, attention, love, gifts, time, and money. We can follow the internal or external voices that advise us to keep our talents hidden, or we can choose to follow our guidance and to bring forth our unique gifts. Within the power of choice lies our ability to apply our will in the co-creational process.

The elements work co-creatively with Spirit, and we can use their ability to do so to help us achieve our desires. Using Air and the mental realm, we can choose to focus our intention on our desire. We can learn to run clear, clean emotional currents, thus charging the Water of our emotional realm with our intention, and aligning thought and feeling. Then, by aligning our inner Fire, our life force and actions, with the thought and feeling of Air and Water, we can connect with Spirit and bring the energies of Spirit into the Earth realm -- matter.

As we begin truly to see ourselves as the divine spark of Spirit we are, we can make choices that are in alignment with our fullness and use our co-creational power effectively. As Divine beings, we contain the power of creation and manifestation within us. In the spiritual realm, with this power comes not only the right to use it but the responsibility to use it wisely. We grow as co-creator each time we use this power wisely for ourselves, for the benefit of humanity, and for all life.

Exercises: Co-Creation

Take a few minutes to meditate, and then ask Spirit to show you a choice you need to make right now to increase your co-creational abilities. As you give thanks for that guidance, allow the deeper, fuller wisdom of that choice to emerge for you. Journal about your experience.

Co-Creational Collage: Gather some magazines, glue, poster board, and scissors to prepare for this exercise. Connect to your essence, and allow your intuition to find pictures and words in magazines that feel exciting or important to you right now. When you feel complete, start pasting them on the board. Just allow your intuition and Spirit to guide you. When you are complete, sit in front of your collage and ask it to give you its messages.

Spirit's Developmental Task

As we recognize ourselves as a spark of Spirit, a spark of Divinity, we begin the quest to connect with our unique essence and to express it in the world. This, along with the conscious co-creation of our own life, represents the developmental task of Spirit.

Our essence, our spark, and the part of Spirit within us make our life and our creations unique. If we go through life without expressing ourselves fully, the part of creation, the aspect of Spirit, that constitutes who we are goes unfilled in the universe. We can visualize this like a giant puzzle where each piece serves as the unique expression of each one of us. With even one piece missing, the puzzle remains incomplete in its full expression.

Many of us forget that our essence -- the puzzle piece we bring -- has tremendous importance in the world. In addition, our essence seeks to express itself and is actually our reason for being. Our purpose in life revolves around expressing ourselves in a way that feels truthful, honest and in alignment with our essence. We need to notice what we are longing to do and to be. What feels like our main drive in life? Have we allowed ourselves to discover our inner motivations and desires, or have we simply followed the dictates of the outer world? What are our secret dreams? We need to allow ourselves to value all that seeks expression through us, because this tells us about how our Spirit wants to express itself.

We want to allow ourselves to unfold, to let our magnificent, radiant selves shine in the world and to create all that we are meant to create; connecting with our essence and expressing it in the world. Just as the elemental forces combined in a certain way to create us, no other person exists with the same essence combination. In turn, we can combine the elemental forces in unique ways to create from our unique Divine spark.

Remember, we are made from the elements. Since they make up who we are, we know them intimately. We want to continue to bring this understanding to conscious awareness and to allow ourselves to express and to create with this knowledge. We want to learn to work with the elements consciously to create our deepest desires so our Spirit can express itself and our Soul can evolve and grow.

To achieve our deepest desires often takes a willingness to move through old fears and feelings of limitation. That's how our desires provide growth. Sometimes growth also requires work. For instance, we may need to develop additional strength, discipline, and determination to grow. Our growth also may require patience, nurturing, and deep caring so we can move through layers of old programming. We have to learn to listen to the signals our Spirit gives us and to do the Soul work we are guided toward. It often takes faith, perseverance, and profound courage to make the personal changes that may be required to move us to the next level in our personal development.

When our Spirit takes growth steps or moves into a new developmental phase, some traditions call these specific periods initiation cycles. Like most cyclic things, such as the moon or the seasons, we naturally change and develop until we reach a peak, and then we begin to devolve or move towards completion. During our lives, we spend some time in growth cycles and others in completion, death, and leaving processes. This can be compared to a forest, which includes trees in all stages of growth, from seeds to saplings, from young trees to mature trees, and from old growth trees to dying trees. So it is with the cycle of our consciousness. If we allow it to change and grow, it will contain all growth levels at the same time. Therefore, we need to become comfortable with the different levels of growth and change happening within.

At the same time, we need to know when to clear out the dead underbrush, if you will, from our mental forest. We may have childhood beliefs that it might be time to release, so we can embrace new concepts and allow them to take root and alter our conscious awareness. Or we might have old feelings we need to clear out so greater feelings of expansion can be seeded within our consciousness. Perhaps we need to let go of old actions, habits, or old ways of being in the world to make room for more life force to flow and help our forest grow. Perhaps we have old things to let go of in the physical world (old clothes, furniture, pictures, and other stuff that keeps us tied energetically to the past) to make room for new seedlings to be planted and to sprout.

Natural Rhythm Cycle: Active and Receptive

At the core of Spirit, Source, or All That Is lies the receptive and active principle. Originally, the expression was genderless and in a constant flowing dance. As we have seen, Source then moved into its next expression, separating into feminine and masculine, both with receptive and active qualities, giving us the image of Spirit as Divine consorts. Here the Divine Feminine resides in balance with the Divine Masculine, God and Goddess in sacred union.

Throughout the ages, we have put labels, names, and definitions on the Divine. Spirit to some has been defined as God, to others as Goddess, to still others as All That Is. This rich substance inhabits everything -- every tree, animal, insect, flower, and human being. Nothing exists without the substance of Spirit flowing through it.

If we try to narrowly define Spirit, we may leave out part of the whole. If we decide that Spirit is a Goddess and that anyone who has a feminine face wears the face of the Divine, and someone else decides that God is Spirit, and anyone who wears a masculine face is an expression of the Divine, we leave out part of the whole, a facet of all that is. For at the core level, Spirit contains both the feminine and the masculine face, Goddess and God.

When we honor both expressions of the Divine and see the Divine in all things, we come into unity consciousness. From this inner container of oneness, we access our compassion for others and our ability to hold the belief that multiple paths to the Divine exist. Just as the Divine couple expresses balance as they work together in sacred union, we are evolving into a balanced view of the Divine that includes both the Divine Feminine and the Divine Masculine, each honored for the part they play in the creation of new life.

Our past has shown us that when we narrowly define Spirit and do not allow others the same privilege, we may end up destroying aspects of the whole -- other people whose beliefs are different than ours. When we look at one facet of something as vast as Spirit, it becomes easy to name one of the parts as its ultimate defining point and claim that facet as the whole, even though, in reality, it remains just a part. Many times people have argued and even killed over their opinion of Spirit. Yet, if we all acknowledge that Spirit is a rich substance with many facets and expressions, we are all correct in our model and can honor one another for our different view points and ways of expressing. As we have already stated, Spirit exists in all things, in all beings, and in all states of evolvement.

The Divine Feminine, the Goddess, has been called by thousands of names and expressions throughout the world. Isis, Gaia, Kuan Yin, Mother Mary, Tara, Pele, Aphrodite, Shakti, Hestia, and Cerridwen represent only a few of the names by which she has been known. The Divine Feminine expressions give women and men a way to more deeply know themselves in connection to the wholeness of all life and to honor the Divine aspect of nurturing and birthing new life.

In different cultures, the Divine Masculine, God, also has many names and expressions. He is called Osiris, YHWH, Allah, Shiva, Jehovah, Vishnu, Odin, Christ, Green Man, and many other names. In many traditions, He is the masculine counter-part to Goddess. The Divine Masculine has a unique expression and provides an important connection for both men and women. While the Divine Feminine nurtures the seed until birth, He is honored as the one that nurtures, grows, and then plants the seed itself. Thus, both God and Goddess have vital functions in creation.

As sparks of the Divine, both women and men have the receptive and active, or the yin and yang, principles within them. The day and night working in union with one another demonstrate these two principles in motion. We need both the active principle of the sun, providing light for the day and outer activity, and the receptive principle of the moon, allowing the dark of the night time to turn inward and rest. Each of us carries and works with both of these principles within.

The yin and yang, feminine and masculine, energies work together and within us in four different ways: masculine yin and feminine yin and masculine yang and feminine yang. The receptive masculine yin energy offers the ability to contain and nurture the seeds of a new creation. The active masculine yang energy brings the ability to expand, penetrate, and plant the new creational seed. The feminine yin represents the place where the seed is nurtured to its fully-developed state, and the birthing energy of the feminine yang brings forth the new creation into the outer world. All four aspects of yin and yang function in our consciousness to bring a new creation fully to the outer world. The energy that is most needed at a particular time takes center stage when it is time to call upon that function.[2]

As we develop the active and receptive principles within and allow them to function in co-creative harmony, we begin to embrace the next level of consciousness, unity and wholeness. The time arrives when we can embody a partnership consciousness -- the ability to work together with one another and within all aspects of the self. At this point, we can bring the active and receptive principles of feminine and masculine balance into our relationships and communities. Now we enter into sacred union with one another and All That Is, utilizing the best of our past, of patriarchy and matriarchy, to create a new partnership frequency with which to enhance our ability to co-create the world of our dreams.

Just as our physical body develops from the infant stage to that of a mature adult, our consciousness evolves and develops over time. Our awareness and our intellect grows, and we learn to think in new ways. We achieve an enormous stage of spiritual development when we fully mature into the ability to know and to honor the multi-faceted nature of Spirit, life, self, and others. It takes a deep level of spiritual maturity to no longer label other expressions of Spirit as good or bad, right or wrong, and to hold all the varied spiritual expressions as part of the whole, as aspects of the Divine.

As we continue to develop spiritually and find ourselves able to sustain the awareness that everything exists as part of Spirit, we continually acknowledge that nothing is separate from Spirit regardless of how it appears in the outer world. Everything is part of the whole. Even destruction of the old remains part of the creation of the new. The deeper our understanding of the whole, the more we understand that each individual's expression and path exists as part of that whole. From this expanded perspective, we develop the ability to have compassion for each other's journey and for our own. This spiritual maturity develops the soul quality of compassion within us and the ability to hold others and ourselves in a state of grace.

In this century, it has become necessary for us to increase our ability to balance the human-made world and the natural world. We are called on as a civilization to harmoniously integrate the two both internally and externally. We are being called to move to the next stage of development -- from dualism to unification. We need to apply unity to our personal consciousness and to the framework that makes up our civilization. As we connect to a greater extent to one another in a global context, our tolerance of people who express a different facet of Spirit becomes even more important. To grow and evolve as a culture, we need room for the variety of people and species on the planet to express themselves and to flourish. This serves as part of the developmental work of the elements. They teach us to honor other paths and choices. The elements remind us that people on different paths may need to practice understanding each other and working in harmony. It takes learning to respect other modalities of learning and being, as well as learning to admire other types of wisdom, to see the true value of all paths.

Additional Spirit Mystery School Teachings

As Above/So Below

In the ancient mystery schools, the priestesses, priests, alchemists, astrologers, and learned ones studied the cosmos to understand the principles of the universe. They believed that the stars, planets, constellations, asteroids, sun, and moon "above" each had a corresponding energy "below" here on Earth. They learned from these energies and applied the principles they discovered as guidance for their lives. The sun and moon present us with the clearest example of this principle, which we call "As Above/So Below" and see clearly as we witness their changing cycles and phases. Both have a growing, outward moving energy and a reflective, inward turning energy. We experience the same principle every day, in our active and rest cycle. The sacred dance of the cosmic forces has much to teach us when we open to learn from the energies above and apply that knowledge to the below life here on Earth.[3]

As Within/So Without

The As Within/So Without principle was also part of the ancient mystery school teachings and shows us how our inner and outer world work together.[4] We serve as the lens through which all our life is viewed. Our beliefs, thoughts, feelings, actions, and personal connection to Spirit are all uniquely ours, and they provide the means by which we see the world. Our outer world continually reflects our inner state of being. And we filter all that happens in our outer world through our inner lens.

We both direct our co-creative energies from the inside out and receive experiences from the outside in. In life, some things are outside our personal conscious control, like the death of a loved one or a disaster in the world. In those types of circumstances, we have the ability to influence our response to them from our inner state of awareness. Each of us learns in this mystery school to develop the capacity to take an outside event and determine our inner response. And, simultaneously, we can use our inner skill to call forth our co-creational powers of alignment to magnetize our desires and dreams in the outer world.

Compassion

As we grow spiritually and develop the ability to sustain the awareness that everything exists as part of Spirit, we begin to see that each individual's expression and path has a place in the greater whole. This gives us a deeper understanding of the whole as well as of each individual. From that perspective, we develop compassion for the journey of others and ourselves. The soul quality of compassion develops in the realm of Spirit when we truly realize the interconnection of all life. With a compassionate heart, we can feel the parts of life that cause suffering and tenderly embrace the world and people around us.

Creativity

When we feel a creative urge, we know Spirit is calling to be expressed through us and we must find a way to open the channel of our creativity. To fully flow through us, Spirit needs us to open this door. The form creativity takes isn't important; it's only important that Spirit can express through us. We can write, paint, dance, sing, garden, cook, decorate, craft; the activity doesn't matter as long as we heed the creative impulse. The more we follow our creative urges, the greater Spirit's expression can come through us.

Stopping this flow by not following Spirit's promptings actually can prove harmful to our health or our life force. Creativity needs to move, and its energy will express through each of us in a distinctive way. Many levels of creativity exist ranging from the purely artistic forms of painting, music, and dance to simply living our lives creatively. We all possess a creative nature and create all the time with each choice of expression we make. Even dressing and choosing the food we eat are creative choices we make every day. And each day we have many opportunities to provide an outlet for Spirit's creative expression within us.

Exercise: Expressing Creativity

In meditation, connect with Spirit and your essence. Ask Spirit where you need to express more creativity in your everyday life. Ask: Do I need a creative outlet? Where am I applying my creativity now? Where else does Spirit want me to express my creativity? Journal about the responses you receive to these questions, and, when you are ready, express your essence in a creative activity.

Grace and Trust

When we allow trust and grace to fill our lives, we find one of the keys to working with Spirit. We must learn to trust our own inner knowing, the still small voice within, and the unfolding process of our own life. Grace moves through our lives as our Soul and Spirit come into alignment and the Divine fully flows through us. We can ask for grace to fill us with the precious magic it brings to life as we deepen our trust in Spirit moving through us.

Life Purpose

Our main life's purpose is not found in a job. It is found in the expression of our Soul, simply expressing what seeks to move through us and allowing our life to develop along this course. That movement may take us through different jobs, homes, locations, relationships, and life expressions. We must remember the importance of connecting to the underlying energy of Spirit not just sometimes but all the time -- as a continual way of being.

Exercise: Life Purpose

Ask Spirit what clues it has for you about the on-going expression of your life's purpose, and journal about Spirit's response to you. Also ask Spirit if there is something you need to know to take your life's purpose to the next level?

Upliftment

Upliftment is the energetic function of lifting energy. Many ways exist to raise the vibration of our lives. Appreciation of anything uplifts our life vibration. So, feeling gratitude offers a wonderful way to achieve upliftment. In addition, simply going out in nature can be extremely uplifting; admiring nature adds to the power of experiencing nature. We can uplift another person by gently placing our energy under them mentally and asking for them to be uplifted.

As we go through our day, we also can start noticing what raises our energy and what lowers it. We need especially to pay attention to what feels uplifting to us, so we can be conscious of adding those things to our daily routine. The more we can keep ourselves in an uplifted state, the more energy we have to apply to our co-creations.

Beloved source of life, Spirit that flows through all things,
thank you for your Divine expression through us.
We appreciate the gifts you bring of choice and co-creation
as tools to create our dreams and desires. Thank you for
uplifting our lives with graceful movement and teaching
us to trust your steps as we dance to your magical pulse.

CHAPTER EIGHT

Elemental Tools

"We ought to dance with rapture

that we might be alive... and part

of the living, incarnate cosmos."

D.H. Lawrence

*A*s dancers proceed in their training, they learn how to pack their dance bags carefully for class or performance. They discover the special, individual tools they each need to help achieve their best performance. They pile into the bag the kinds of shoes they love for each type of dance, their make-up, hair kit, costume pieces, emergency items, band aids, pain relievers, ointments, ice-packs, and the food and drink necessary to fuel all that movement. Dance bags usually weigh a lot, yet they are filled with the essentials for dancing well and for the dancers personal self-care.

As you learn to dance with the rhythms of nature, you too will want to have a bag of tools handy. Part of your co-creational journey requires learning which elemental skill you need to use and when, because each elemental realm needs different approaches to work effectively. This chapter provides you with tools and handy references for boosting your connection to the elements and allowing them to assist you in the creation of your desires. Use them any time in your co-creational journey.

Clearing Tools

Each element possesses powerful means for clearing energy and balancing and harmonizing you when you are feeling out of sorts or drained by an environment you have been in. When working with the elements, always remember that your intention moves the energy. The clearer your intention, plan, or purpose, the more success you will achieve with the process you engage. As with any of your work with the elements, you want to remember to thank them for their assistance when you complete any energetic process.

Earth Clearing:

Peruvian Shaman's have a slightly different way of looking at energy than many Westerners. Instead of qualifying energy as positive or negative, good or bad, light or dark, they talk about energy in terms of density. Energy that appears dense to one person may actually seem lighter to another. It all depends on the person's sensitivity level and development.

According to their tradition, *Pachamama*, the Earth Mother, uses your dense energy as food. Anytime you release your dense energy into the earth, she transforms it into nourishment for herself.

You can use Earth for energetic clearing in many ways. For instance, go out in nature, and stand on *Pachamama*. Using intention consciously, ask that your body be filled with lighter vibrations from Spirit. Breathe in the light vibrations of Spirit until you sense a feeling of fullness. Then ask your body to drain any dense energy into the earth, allowing the lighter vibrations to fully fill your body. Imagine that you have filled a straw with liquid and held it trapped by placing your finger at the top of the straw. You then remove your finger, thus the releasing the liquid so it could drain out the bottom of the straw. After releasing the dense energy, generally you feel much lighter.[1]

You also can clear with Earth by ceremonially burying something you are ready to release. You could create a simple ceremony for yourself to bury an old ring when a relationship ends or bury any meaningful or symbolic item when you need to let go of an old energy.

Water Clearing:

Before entering a body of water for bathing, showering, or swimming, ask the water to clear whatever you are ready to release. You can charge the water to do any other type of emotional release work needed. You can add things to the water, such as apple cider vinegar, sea salt, baking soda, or Epsom salts to provide additional clearing power.

Crying also provides a water-clearing tool. When you cry, your tears release emotions, sometimes at a very deep soul level.

Additionally, you can release old energies to the current traveling downstream in a creek or river and open to an influx of the new when you turn to face upstream.

Air Clearing:

You can use any of Air's vibrational modalities with the intention to clear the energy in a room, a home, a business, or in yourself. Meditation, toning, playing a crystal bowl, singing, flower essences, visualization, crystals, and oils, can all be used with the intention to clear energy fields. Burning sage, copal, sweetgrass or incense clear energy through the Air realm and are often referred to as smudging. You also can use the power of word or the vibration of colors to soothe and balance your energy field, bringing you into harmony and alignment.

Fire Clearing:

To use Fire for energy clearing, write down on a piece of paper what you want to clear or transform. Then burn the paper in a fire with the intention of having Fire transmute the energy. Burning an old object with the intention of transforming or clearing the energy associated with it also serves as a powerful clearing tool.

Dance, another Fire tool, gets the life-force moving for any type of clearing work. Simply state your intention for energetic clearing before you begin dancing, and then allow the energy to flow fully in your body while you dance. The emotion of anger is stored in the liver, and the liver loves movement. Dance provides a valuable way to release any deep feelings from the body. The more you actually allow your body to move in the way it wants, the more you clear your energy.

Spirit Clearing:

In the realm of Spirit, you need to call on the support of the invisible world to come to your energy-clearing aid. Prayer serves as a beautiful and powerful tool to use for clearing with Spirit. Often the greatest clearing comes from a prayer for forgiveness. Ask to be forgiven for any ill thoughts, deeds, or words you have had toward anyone including yourself, and follow this by sending love and gratitude to the person.

You also can request clearing assistance from any divine archetype. You can call on assistance from general Divinity, such as God or Goddess, or you can call on a specific aspect of Divinity, such as Kwan Yin, Christ, or Buddha. As you pray, however, remember that the more you feel your prayer request has been answered, the more powerful it becomes. Remember also to give thanks. Responses to prayers often come in dreamtime.You may be guided in your dreams to take certain actions to complete your clearing.

If you find yourself in need of additional ways to work with the elements for clearing or energizing anything in your life and you are unsure of how to accomplish this, spend some time in nature. Spend as much time in the natural world as possible until you feel clear internally about how to proceed. The more deeply you attune to nature, the easier it becomes for you to connect to your inner nature and to find the answer to your questions. Practice using the elements for clearing, and notice the difference in how you feel.

Altars for the Elements

You can work consciously with the elements to support your life and your process of transformation by placing them on an altar and including them in ceremony. An altar in your home or office helps you to focus your energy on working with the elements with intent, and acts as a focal point for your awareness during ceremonies. Consciously calling on the elements in ceremony gives your ritual strength and includes all the realms.

Here are some tips on how to create a ceremonial or personal altar. Start building an altar by choosing a piece of fabric for the altar cloth. Choose a cloth with personal meaning because it represents the fabric of life and the interweaving of all the threads that make up who you are. Place it on the table or surface where you plan to create your altar.

Then choose something to represent each of the elements: Earth, Water, Air, and Fire. A basic altar can be created with simple but meaningful objects, such as a rock for Earth, a shell for Water, a feather for Air, and a candle for Fire. An animal totem altar provides another option. Choose an animal to represent each realm. For instance, a four-legged creature that walks close to the earth like a lion, buffalo, or bear, can symbolize the element of Earth. Water can be represented by a fish, dolphin, or whale. Air by any type of bird, from a simple finch to an eagle, or perhaps by something else that flies, such as a bat or a butterfly. Fire totems include snakes, lizards, and salamanders.

For a more mystical altar, try gnomes for Earth, water sprites or mermaids for Water, fairies or angels for Air, and a dragon for Fire. To create an altar with everyday objects choose salt, grains, bread, or a plant for Earth, a beautiful vessel containing water for Water, sage or incense for Air, and chili peppers for Fire.

Place these on your altar cloth. Once each of the elements are in place, choose something to symbolize Spirit, or the essence of Spirit within you. This could be a religious or spiritual representation of a Divine being, a photograph of yourself, or something you create to represent your inner essence.

Exercise: Altar Building

Notice what type of altar you are feeling drawn to build at this time. Then, begin creating an altar of your own. Take the time to enjoy the process of creating an altar that is a reflection of you. Keep the energy of the altar alive by changing or cleaning it when you need uplifting.

Ceremony

Ceremony connects the outer world with your inner world and gives you a safe place to honor transitions and passages from one cycle or phase of your life to the next. Ceremony assists you in developing your deeper personal connection to the Divine. As you consciously call forth your connection to Spirit during your ceremonial time and place, you create more significance and meaning to those moments in life. You can use ceremony to honor the changes of the seasons or to consciously honor life transitions. For example, you can use ceremony to honor the transition from puberty to adulthood, individual or couple to parent, adult to elder, single to married, or marriage to divorce. You can use ceremony to mark the transition into a new home, a loss or death -- any time or place in life when you feel an internal or external transition needs to be honored.

Ceremony can be done in private or group settings, and the more you involve all the participants in the ceremony itself, the more alive it becomes. As many ways to perform ceremony exist as there are people to do them. For those just beginning their ceremonial exploration, the following guide can be used as a starting point.

Basic Ceremonial Structure

• Determine the intention of the ceremony.

• Determine the place where you will hold the ceremony and who will participate.

• Determine the ceremonial structure. If appropriate in the body of the ceremony, include all elemental realms. You can do this in the following ways:...

Earth: Include an activity that involves the body -- something physical to do within the ceremony, such as a movement prayer or dancing to embody a principle or concept of the ceremony.

Water: Include something within the ceremony to create a safe space for being with or communicating feelings or emotions.

Air: Include an activity that sets an intention for creation or a release exercise that works with changing a belief system or a meditation that elevates the vibration of the participants.

Fire: Raise the life force of the group with energy-invoking music, dancing, drumming, and/or singing something the group loves.

Spirit: Honor Spirit by using it as the foundational energy for setting the ceremonial intention. Have an active portion of the ceremony and a receptive (reflective) phase. Bring Spirit into all aspects of ceremony. Direct the ceremonial energy outward for the good of the planet or to the healing of someone or something.

• Energetically clear the ceremonial space by smudging, toning, playing uplifting music, burning incense, etc.

• Prepare the ceremonial space with all the items needed for the ceremony, including a ceremonial altar.

• If needed, energetically clear the participants' energy fields before beginning the ceremony by smudging, or misting with a rosemary, sage, or cedar spray.

• To begin the ceremony "call in" sacred space with the elements and Spirit (See the end of this chapter for suggestions on how to do this.)

• Do the ceremony.

• Close the ceremony with gratitude

• Leave the ceremonial site in as good or better condition than before the ceremony.[2]

Examples: I created a ceremony around abundance for one Summer Solstice, since that constitutes one of the primary teachings of the season. One of the key elements I included in the ceremony was an "a-bun-dance" to call abundance into our lives. This proved not only sacred but great fun!

One Imbolc, the time between Winter Solstice and Spring Equinox, a group of friends and I conducted a networking ceremony. At this seasonal time we traditionally choose additional seeds we want to plant in our lives for the growing season, and we applied that to our professional lives. In our ceremony, each of us spoke about our professions and shared business cards with the intention of sowing a more abundant work season for the upcoming growing cycle through networking.

Suggestion: For those of you who want to work with ceremony in your lives but are unfamiliar with the art, you could begin by reading books on earth-based spirituality. They include many ceremonial suggestions: try some of the ones you feel comfortable with. You might also find a group of people who currently do seasonal ceremonies and celebrations, and attend one. You want to be in ceremony with people with whom you feel safe and comfortable. Maybe someone in your area offers a course on ceremony and celebration. A wonderful earth-based course of study can deeply enrich your life.

If you want to include dance when you work with the energy of the elements within your ceremony, you might try a spinning or tribal dance for Earth, a flowing dance for Water, a freedom dance for Air, an intense dance for Fire, and a dance to spiritually inspiring music for Spirit.

Ceremony serves as a powerful container for energy, so it is important to create ceremonial environments that deeply enrich the lives of the participants. Remember to have fun and create each ceremony with purposeful intent, joy, and reverence for the sacred in all life.

Calling in Sacred Space

It is important that ceremony be done in a consciousness container of sacredness. To invoke that container of conscious awareness, call in sacred space. When you choose the energies of consciousness that you want to be present in your ceremony, and call them forth either silently or out loud, you are "calling in sacred space." Ceremony needs to be done in a manner that honors and respects all the energies called in, as well as the participants.

To call in sacred space for your ceremony, you can call on the element of Earth to bring you such things as groundedness, good health, a happy home, fertility, strength, gratitude, and abundance. You can ask Earth to teach you to honor the sacredness of the beloved planet and your precious body and to help you seek knowledge and wisdom from nature.

From Water, you can request emotional support, feeling guidance, clear intuition, friendship, understanding, and good relationships. You can ask Water to bathe you in love, to sustain and nurture you, to increase flow in your life, to teach you to give as well as to receive, as well as to rejuvenate and regenerate you.

To call on Air, you may ask for vibrational attunement, wisdom, good communication, increased ability to listen, intellectual growth, knowledge, swift thinking, clear sight, and knowing.

Calling on the power of Fire, you may request transformation in some area of your life, healthy sexual expression, passion, personal power, ambition, warmth, joy, and life force.

And for Spirit, you can call on any aspect of the Divine with which you resonate -- God, Goddess, Spirit, All That Is, or individual deities such as Gaia, Green Man, Isis, Osirus, Christ, Mary, Kwan Yin, Buddha, Tara, or any Divine being that you choose to work with energetically. You also can call on Spirit to bring the energy of creativity, compassion, balance, and spiritual growth.

Many more ways exist for calling in the elements; choose those that feel good and appropriate for each particular ceremony. The energy with which you approach the elements is important. You need to invoke them with a pure heart and intention, as well as respecting and honoring them for the powerful forces they are. Remember to thank the elements for working with you when you complete your ceremony.

Calling in the Elemental Forces

The following represent some examples of concepts that can be called in with each element.

Earth
  The Power of Earth

  The Physical Realm

  Your Body

  Groundedness

  Good Health

  A Happy Home

  Fertility in all or certain aspects of our lives

  Strength

  Gratitude

  Abundance

  Rhythms of Life

  Honor the sacredness of our beloved Earth and our precious bodies

  Knowledge from Nature

  Animals that walk on four legs

  Gnomes

  Astrological Archetypes of Taurus, Virgo and Capricorn

Water   *The Power of Water*

The Feeling and Emotional Realm

Emotional Support

Intuition

Clear Emotions

Friendship

Understanding

Good Relationships

Being Bathed in Love

Allowing Life to Flow

Sustainability

Birthing Waters

Ebb and Flow

Giving and Receiving

Feeling Guidance

Fluidity

Rejuvenation and Regeneration

Water Sprites

Dolphins, Whales, Fish, and Water creatures

Astrological Archetypes of Cancer, Scorpio, and Pisces

Air

The Power of Air

The Mental Realm

Vibrational Attunement

Wisdom

Good Communication

Clean Air

The Ability to Listen

Breath of Life

Intellectual Growth

Knowledge

Intention

Clear Thinking

Clarity

Perspective

Knowing

Power of Prayer

Meditation

Fairies

Angels

Winged Ones

Astrological Archetypes of Gemini, Libra, and Aquarius

Fire   *The Power of Fire*

The Action Realm

Passion

Transformation

Sexuality

Illumination

Ambition

Ecstasy

Right Use of Power

Joy

Living Fully

Life-Force

Warmth

Energy

Will

Movement

Dragons

Snakes

Phoenix

Astrological Archetypes of Aries, Leo, and Sagittarius

Spirit   *The Power of Spirit*

God and Goddess

Divine Masculine

Divine Feminine

Essence Expression

Personal Responsibility

Grace and Trust

Desire

Sacred Union

Life Purpose

Upliftment

Unified Field

Creativity

Compassion

Balance

Spiritual Growth

Guides and Teachers

Yin and Yang

Receptive and Active Energies

Personal Divinity and Humanity

Sun and Moon

Examples of Acknowledging the Directions
& Elements for Calling in Sacred Space

1. (EAST)

We invite the direction of the East and the element of Fire - the action realm - to our circle. With Fire we activate new beginnings, our passion, sexuality, vitality, and growth. We honor the power of transformation and purification. We call on the Fire realm beings: dragons, snakes, and the phoenix. We invoke the power of the sun, light, life-force energy, and our Radiant Selves. We connect with our ambition, ecstasy, warmth, and joy. We ask to grow in wisdom as we shine the light of awareness on our inner world. We claim the power of our actions and align them with the highest good for all.

2. (SOUTH)

We invite the direction of the South and the element of Water - the emotional realm - to our circle. With Water we activate our emotional maturity and ask to have the wisdom to respond, instead of to react, to life. We ask that our emotional realm be clear, clean, and current. We invite the spirit of the lakes, rivers, streams, oceans, and rain to join us. We invite the dolphins, whales, fish, mermaids, and water sprites to our circle. We honor our inner child, the deep teachings of the mirror of relationships, and the potency of regeneration. We activate and align the Water power of love with the highest good for all.

3. (WEST)

We invite the direction of the West and the element of Air - the mental realm - to our circle. With Air we activate the precious gift that the breath of life gives us. We ask to hear our inner voice of wisdom. We activate our ability to consciously set the vibrational tone of our lives. We ask to see the cosmic and archetypal perspective of our personal and mass consciousness belief systems. We open to deep listening to one another. As we call on the birds and the winged ones, we ask for the courage to be the visionaries for our time. We call on the angelic realm and all those who assist us on the inner realm to guide our path. We claim the Air power of intention and align our intentions with the highest good of all.

4. (NORTH)

We invite the direction of the North and the element of Earth - the physical realm - to our circle. With Earth we activate our ability to gain inner knowledge from our connection to nature. We ask to embody wholeness with Spirit fully connected to our bodies, and for constant awareness of the sacredness of all life. We ask to hear the deep wisdom of our body as it assists us in maintaining good health. We learn to structure sustainable foundations and earth-centered systems. We call on bear, cats, dogs, horses, and all four-legged creatures that walk the earth in harmony with her rhythm. As we develop the soul quality of gratitude, may Earth share with us her guidance on fertility and abundance so we may become grounded in all endeavors. As we activate the power to stand on our own, may we be aligned with the highest good for all.

5. (CENTER)

We invite the direction of Center and Spirit to our circle. We honor both the Divine Feminine and Divine Masculine. We activate the As Above/So Below Mysteries and the As Within/So Without Mysteries. We call on the deep wisdom of the yin and yang, receptive and active forces. We ask to align the forces within toward inner balance, allowing the wisdom and rhythm of the sun and moon to guide our own lives. We call on all those connected to sacred union: Goddess and God, Magdalene and Christ, Gaia and Green Man, Isis and Osirus, Shakti and Shiva. We call forth our own inner essence and ask that our expression in the world be toward the highest good of all. May we use our power of choice wisely, and may we have compassion for all life. May we grow in our ability to activate a unified field of awareness, bringing forth our Spirit filled desires with grace and ease.

Honoring Prayers and Blessings

Writing and speaking your own prayers and blessings to the forces of nature enriches you and honors them. I've provided one example of a prayer and a blessing for each element.

 **Exercise: Creating Prayers and Blessings**
Create your own prayer and blessing for each element. If you feel inspired to do so, make a collage to honor each element.

Earth Honoring Prayer

*Precious Earth, the beauty of your nature uplifts
and nourishes our bodies and souls.
The majesty of your mountains reminds us
to structure and form our lives.
You remind us to take solid, grounded steps
as we build firm foundations with gratitude.*

*Through your ability to contain, you give us the ability
to walk, skip, and dance.
You teach us to celebrate the gift of our bodies
and the treasures of the physical realm.
With you, we are able to touch our loved ones
and to feel the tenderness of a kiss.*

*We open to embody wholeness as we learn to honor
the sacred in your realm.
You train us to value the deep wisdom of the body
and to tend to its needs.
Thank you for your cycles which help us align
with the organic timing of change.*

Earth Blessing

*Earth, with deep reverence we ask that (name or this being, this
couple, this organization) be blessed by you with the ability
to have a solid foundation in all that they bring forth.
May they be graced with Earth-honoring abundance and fertility
that ripens into a harvest so bountiful that they need to share it.*

Water Honoring Prayer

Sweet Water, thank you for your precious nourishment.
Your essence quenches our soul's longing for love.
You bring moisture to all our dry places
with your never-ending wellspring of feelings.

You soften the ground we walk upon
and bring forth the flowering of our being.
It is you that cleanses the body temple
as you wash away our inner doubts.
You bring the richness of relationship
and help us to see our reflection in the mirror of others.

Next to you, oh great and holy Water,
we feel the rejuvenation of Source.
Our hearts lift up in gratitude for how you
create the fertile ground of life.
We honor you and sing your praises...blessed be sweet Water.

Water Blessing

Water, in gratitude we ask that (name or this being,
this couple, this organization) be blessed by you
with an over-flowing sea of love.
May the lives of all those who come into contact
with (her/him/them) be enhanced by their abundance of love.

Air Honoring Prayer

Beloved Air, you bring us the breath of life
and the gift of peace through perspective.
Thank you for teaching us to focus our mental energy
through the power of intention
and for bringing the integration of whole-brain thinking,
creativity, and sequencing.
Through your tools of meditation and prayer,
we are able to call on our ethereal allies.
Our angels, guides, teachers, and archetypes
then become able to assist us.
As we free our beliefs from mass consciousness,
we find our visionary capacity.

You bring the ability to clear our old energetic cords
and belief systems
so we can choose thoughts and words
that uplift our lives.
Thank you for the ability to communicate
our unique vibration through you.

Air Blessing

Air, with appreciation we ask that (name or this being,
this couple, this organization) be blessed by you with the ability
to honor others' viewpoints and perspectives.
Grace them with the capacity to hold a vision of peace.
Show them how to work with you to focus their intention
so they may bring forth their desires and dreams
and uplift their vibration.

Fire Honoring Prayer

Oh, immense Fire of illumination,
thank you for shining your light on our lives.
You bring us the ability to see what was previously hidden
and to travel to unseen realms.
You bring the spark of life that activates growth
and develops a strong life force.
Your dynamic energy fuels our Radiant Self
when we are connected to our passions.
Through your power of action, we are able to move
our lives toward growth.
We honor the wisdom of your light/dark cycle
as we learn to balance our activity and rest.

Through you, we learn to let go of old forms
to allow full transformation to occur.
By your side, we warm ourselves
and connect to our sexuality and sensuality.
We are grateful for our right use of will
which allows us to use our power with wisdom.

Fire Blessing

Fire, with profound admiration, we ask that (name or this being,
this couple, this organization) be blessed by your energizing
warmth and life force as they take action in their lives.
We ask that all those who come into contact with (her/him/them)
be illuminated by their expression of your radiant passion.

Spirit Honoring Prayer

Great Spirit, source of all that is,
thank you for the blessing and gift of our lives.
Your essence moves through all realms
and teaches us the interconnectedness of all life.
From you we learn to take personal responsibility
for the spark of Divinity that we are.

You train us to use the power of choice
to co-create our lives with harmony and grace.
Through you, we discover how to express our essence
and to live our life's purpose.
You show us the importance of being both active and receptive.
We are grateful for the wisdom of the as above/so below mysteries
as we learn to honor all realms.
You show us how to enhance our inner realm
and to become uplifting to those around us.
We ask that you help us hold a unified field of co-creation in
harmony and alignment through our sacred union with you.

Spirit Blessing

Dearest Spirit, we ask that (name or this being,
this couple, this organization) be blessed with an abundant grace
and trust in life, even during times of transformation and change.
May the lives of all those who come into contact with (her/him/
them) be uplifted by their connection to the Divine
and their deep compassion for the sacredness
of the human experience.

CHAPTER NINE

Sacred Timings

"Dance is for everybody.

I believe that the dance came from the people

and that it should always be delivered

back to the people."

Alvin Ailey

$\mathcal{N}$ature's sacred timings provide the rhythmic music for your life's co-creational dance. The deeper your alignment with her pulse and tempo, the more gracefully and easily you bring your desires into being. Indeed, your awareness of the sacred natural rhythms helps you time each phase of your co-creations so you bring your desires into manifestation as if part of a well-orchestrated and choreographed dance.

Aligning yourself with Spirit, the elements, and the natural rhythms of nature helps you bring your desires into form. For your co-creational dance to become effortless and graceful, you need to learn to coordinate it and to choreograph it one step at a time. You wouldn't ask yourself to learn ballet in a few lessons or by simply reading a book about it. You would expect to work with the skills over time and to practice regularly. Proficiency in ballet takes approximately ten years of good training and practice. As with classical dance, if you expect too much too soon from your ability to coordinate your co-creational dance, you may become frustrated and give up. Only when you fall in love with the practice itself, when you learn to value being able to move with grace and ease, or when you want to dance so badly that you are unwilling to give up until you develop the skill, will you stick with the practice long enough to fully learn to dance -- or in this case, to co-create by dancing to the rhythms of nature.

Patience and regular practice provide the keys to a successful co-creational dance. Just as you would study any dance form, in co-creational dance you learn to hold all the elements together in a unified field -- in your body -- while dancing to the rhythm, the natural rhythms of the universe. A good dance teacher shows students how to move their bodies, teaches them about timing their steps to the music, and then lets them practice doing the steps in time to the music. The student practices moving slowly in the beginning, picking up speed or adding more steps only once they become comfortable doing the first steps they learned. The same holds true for the co-creational dance. You must take what you have learned and begin practicing slowly and mindfully.

In dance, one of the basic lessons involves learning to tune into the music and become aware of its connection to your movements. Your awareness of the music helps you to know when to take your first dance step -- when to begin. Only by listening to the music do you also know when to change your dance to accommodate a shift in rhythm and when to finish your dance and take a deep breath of completion. In the same way, learning to dance to the rhythms of nature requires listening to and increasing your awareness of her sacred timings.

As the sun and the moon travel around the Astrological Wheel and the Wheel of the Year, we are affected by the subtle changes they create in the natural rhythms. For example, have you ever wondered why you may feel the urge to spend time with family and friends during the December holidays, or why you may want to set goals and make resolutions on New Year's Eve, or why diet becomes the major topic of conversation on January 2nd? All of these are brought about by the energetic influence of the Winter Solstice, which occurs between December 20 and 22 each year as the sun moves into the archetype of Capricorn. Capricorn's focus revolves around your responsible connection to your family and friends and how you want to structure your life for the next growing cycle. That structure requires measurable goals and objectives for achieving growth and includes taking care of the earthly realm -- your body.

Prior to entering Capricorn, the sun resides in Sagittarius, the great expander. Thus, if you are unconscious of the true purpose of Sagittarius, as you prepare for the holidays and the New Year you might express the Sagittarius Fire of expansion externally and to excess. You might spend too much on your holiday purchases, eat and drink too much at parties, and burn yourself out with too much activity, all of which give you good reasons to diet, budget, and structure once the sun moves into Capricorn.

If you understand the Fire of Sagittarius, however, you know that it needs to be balanced with inner time for exploration. Instead of overindulging and expressing yourself in excessive ways, you will take time during the darkest days of the year to go into your inner terrain to investigate where the spark of new life burns for you. You will ask yourself

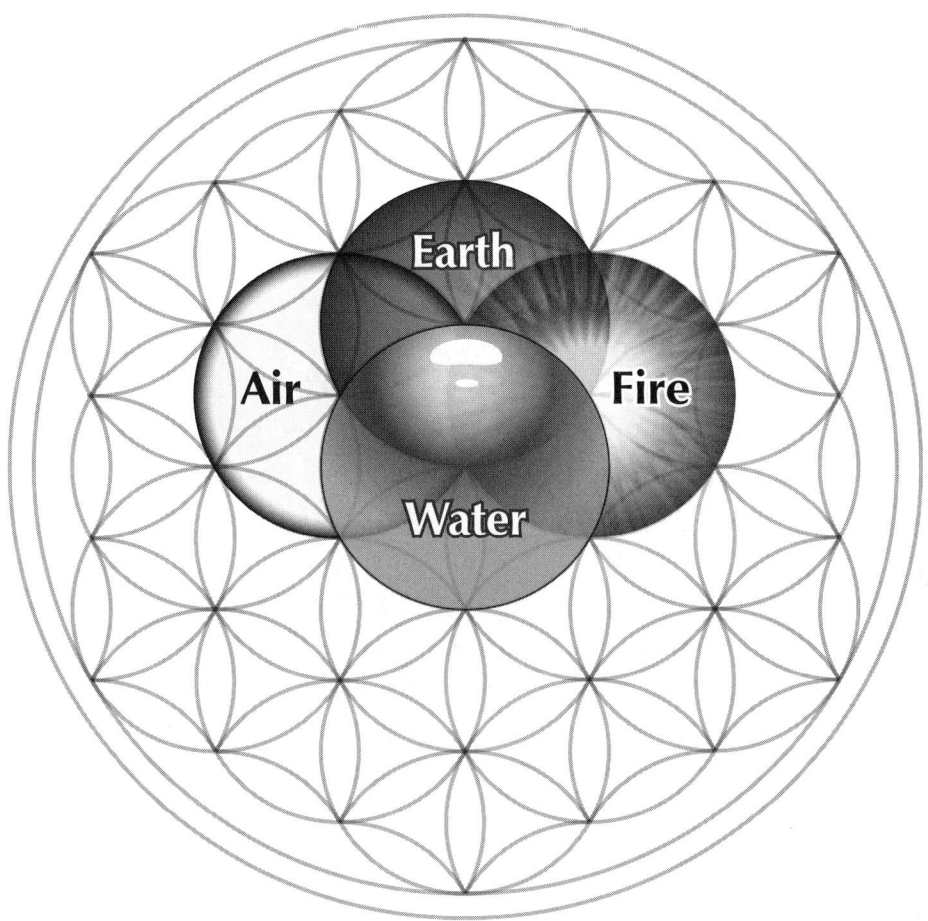

what you want to bring forth in the new growing cycle, and the goals you form for the New Year come from your deepest inner knowing, ready to be co-created.

Becoming more aware of the ways the subtle changes in energy happen throughout the year, month, and day can help you line up with those energies and use them the most effectively. Then the celestial music of the spheres -- the sun, moon and stars -- can add harmony to the movement of your life. As you begin practicing this process you will start by learning to work with the individual elements like you would learn to move your arms, legs, head, and feet slowly and separately in classical ballet. At this point, you can begin working with them all together in a unified field, like a dancer moving his or her entire body in a coordinated fashion. As those skills develop, you also can practice moving to the various rhythms and timings that nature provides through the Wheel of the Year, the moon, the astrological gates of awareness and the daily light and dark cycle, gracefully learning to dance your co-creations into being with harmonic synergy.

Coordinating Your Unified Field

To coordinate your co-creative dance effectively, you need to practice aligning all the elements and Spirit into a unified field in your body, the physical meeting place of your Spirit, emotions, mind, and actions. To get an idea what this entails, imagine that you are a dancer. Before you possess the capacity to perform a ballet step with full bodily coordination, you must go down a checklist in your mind to make sure you are prepared to start that particular step. You review the step, making sure you remember how to do it. You double check that your body is held correctly -- shoulders down, ribs in, feet in the right position, etc. You look around you to be sure you have enough space to perform the movement and to be certain you know in which direction to turn your body. Now, you are ready to move and actually perform the ballet step to the music.

Apply this same process to your unified field until it becomes effortless, like a well-practiced dance step.

Before beginning your co-creative process, you want to coordinate your unified field. In this case, your checklist involves mentally running through the elements, including Spirit, before you start moving to the music -- the natural rhythms.

Spirit: Describe the essence idea you want to bring into form with as much clarity as possible at the moment.

Air: State your intention and commit to the focus needed to complete it.

Water: Call forth the feeling of the idea completely fulfilled and hold that feeling in the body. Clearing may be needed if the frequency of completion cannot be held in the emotional realm.

Fire: Define the actions needed and connect to as much energy and passion for the creation as possible.

Earth: Anchor the unified field in the physical realm through dance and by putting it in writing and/or creating an artistic expression.

Remember that sometimes you need to go back and review all the parts of a step or element to increase your awareness. In fact, reviewing the various elements, powers, and skills as you go along helps the process become effortless. Once your abilities increase and you choose to continue growing, life naturally brings you to the next level of expansion. The elements know where you are in your development and guide you to your current learning edge, thus helping you to strengthen the skills you need to continue progressing.

As you begin timing your dance to nature's rhythms, you can choose how quickly or how slowly -- in what time measurements -- you complete your co-creations. It helps most people to begin by going slowly and taking steady steps that become easier with each practice. Some of nature's timings offer a window of opportunity during which you can connect with the energy, so you have concentrated time to practice dancing with it and integrating its energies into your life. For example, each Wheel of the Year point, and the new and full moons, are energetically active for that day, the day before and the day after; they provide these energetic windows of opportunity. (You can find out when the timings occur by logging onto www.naturalrhythms.org and printing out a handy yearly reference guide.)

Rhythms

First Rhythm: Wheel of the Year

The first natural rhythm consists of the eight points on the Wheel of the Year, which fall approximately six weeks apart. If you are just starting your co-creative dance to the natural rhythms and still feel a bit unsure of the steps, you may want to slow your movements to half time and only pay attention only to the solstices and equinoxes, which occur approximately every twelve weeks. Later when you feel secure on the dance floor, you can add in the cross quarter days, which contain even more elemental energy for your dance.

Half Tempo

Winter Solstice gives birth to the seeds you want to bring forth in the coming growing cycle. To take advantage of its energy, you simply can make a list of the dreams and desires you want to co-create in the year ahead, date the list, and place the list in a special place or in your journal. The process of writing can be equated with planting the seeds themselves.

Additionally, you can create a collage or a piece of art depicting those desires. You can perform a ceremony or do a dance to anchor your essence ideas in the physical world. Additionally you can use divinatory cards or tools to discover guidance on your preparations for the upcoming cycle.

Spring Equinox brings a burst of energy that can be used for your co-creations. This represents another good time to tune into where you are in the co-creative process and to journal about your discoveries. Remember to date your journal entries so you can reference them later as you evaluate your co-creational journey. At this point, you can add art, guidance from divination tools, or ceremony to whatever you decide to do as part of your focus on the natural rhythm of creation and growth. Here the light and dark come into balance, so you will want to notice if you need to balance anything in your life in order to bring your desires into being.

Summer Solstice completes the cycle of growing light as we slowly begin our journey to the Wheel's harvest portion. Once again you want to tune into your desires to see if they are moving closer to physical form. Summer Solstice represents a good time to discover what they need to help them come to fruition. More Air focus? More Fire action or energy? More grounded Earth realm attention or Water's love and nurturing? More guidance from Spirit? At this point, you again want to tune into the state of your desire and journal about your discoveries, dating the entry. You can add art, guidance from divination tools, and/or ceremony to your rhythmic process.

Autumnal Equinox serves as a harvest point for your co-creations. At this time of year you evaluate how you did bringing your intentions forth. Once more it is time to tune into the state of your desires, journal about your discoveries, dating the entries, and possibly adding art, guidance from divination tools, or ceremony to your process. Again, the light and dark have come into balance, and you want to notice if there is anything you need to balance in your life as you close the cycle.

Tuning into these four points will give you a nice, slow rhythm for dancing with your creational capabilities. When and if you are ready to pick up the pace, you can add the cross-quarter days into your repertoire.

Full Tempo

Samhain begins the darkest days of the cycle at the time of reaping your final harvest with gratitude and looking back over the last growing cycle. On this day you want to make any notes about how you plan to work with the energy during the year ahead. It is important to go into the inner realm to discover what wants to be birthed during the next cycle. So you should plan to spend some time in reflection during the next six weeks. During that time, you want to journal about your discoveries and date those journal entries. You can add art, guidance from divination tools, or ceremony to your process.

Winter Solstice - see half-tempo section

Imbolc denotes the point when the seeds you planted at Winter Solstice begin to stir. At this point of the Wheel, you want to ask yourself if there are more seeds you want to add to your creational mix to assist in its growing cycle. Take time here for renewal and rejuvenation so you will have the energy you need as spring bursts forth. Journal about your discoveries and date those journal entries. You can add art, guidance from divination tools, or ceremony to help mark this day.

Spring Equinox - see half-tempo section

Beltane marks the time when the energy swells into ripeness. Again, you want to check on your co-creations to see how their growth is progressing. Is there anything they need to make them more fertile? Do they need more Spirit, Air, Water, Fire, or Earth to bring them into form? Journal your discoveries and date those journal entries, and then, if you want you can add art, guidance from divination tools, or ceremony.

Summer Solstice - see half-tempo section

Lughnasad or Lammas, the first of the three harvest points, brings you to a place of gratitude. You ask yourself now what you have to be thankful for in life and in relation to our co-creations. List all those things in your journal. Also ask yourself what desires have come into form and are now ripe and ready for picking. What do you need to add to continue having a good harvest? Journal about your discoveries and date the entries. You can add art, guidance divination tools, or ceremony to mark this point on the Wheel.

Autumnal Equinox - see half-tempo section

Second Rhythm: Moon Cycle

The second natural rhythm is created over the course of a month with thirteen full lunar cycles a year. Again, if you are just starting your co-creational dance to the natural rhythms and still feel a bit unsure of the steps, you may want to slow your timing work down to half tempo, by initially only paying attention to the new moons approximately every twenty-eight and a half days. You can add in the full moons when and if you feel ready.

Thirteen times a year the sun and moon line up at the new moon in the same astrological sign. For example, New Moon in Leo appears only when the sun is in Leo. Since this timing involves both of the major forces that affect Earth, each new moon gives you special, potent archetypal energy for your co-creations. The sun and moon travel through the astrological archetypes throughout the month and the year and come into alignment in the same sign thirteen times each year. When you work with this alignment, you are working with the wheels of the moon (Water), sun (Fire), Earth (earthly realm), and astrology (Air), with the active/receptive Spirit flowing throughout, a very powerful combination.

The sun resides in each astrological gate for approximately thirty days, although the exact date of this occurrence changes slightly from year to year due to leap year. The moon changes signs approximately every two and a half days. In relation to the sacred timings of your creations, you want to pay attention to the archetype where the new moon resides, because that particular energy can be used with your co-creations each month. For example, a new moon in Virgo is a good time to organize the details of your life, get things in order, and develop a plan for your work. A new moon in Pisces allows you to develop a deeper level of compassion for yourself and others, and be of service to the collective.

Just like the darkest days on the Wheel of the Year, the darkest days of the month -- the dark of the moon right before the new moon -- provide the best times for deep inner work to uncover what is ready to come forth. Then, when the next cycle begins - the birth - you are ready to consciously energize those seeds. The birth of the new solar cycle begins at Winter Solstice and the lunar cycle rebirth happens at the new moon.

You can add co-creational energy for your desires at any new moon. You can give them extra energy by aligning your intentions with the current astrological archetype energy of the sun and moon. But, you want to pay attention to the elemental intent of the moon first, to discover if the moon is associated with Fire, Earth, Air or Water. A Fire new moon provides an especially good time for adding energy and fuel to your co-creations, starting new projects, sparking new life in old projects, or taking outer-world action on your intentions. Earth new moons are good for grounded activities. During an Earth new moon you want to anchor your intentions in the physical realm by taking care of your home, garden, body, finances, and business. A new moon in Air signs tells you to pay attention to your focus, notice where your are placing your mental energy, explore your new ideas, and communicate or network about your intentions. A Watery new moon means it is time to attend to your emotional realm, apply love to your intentions, align your feelings, and rejuvenate yourself. After you have aligned your intentions with the element, you can then add the next layer by working with the astrological archetype itself.

You can use the energy of the new moon to help you co-creationally in many ways. You can do something as simple as keeping a journal of your new moon intentions, and then take a few minutes on each new moon to update and connect with the intention. You can add an elemental card reading from the *Elemental Forces of Creation Oracle* to your divination work each month to receive a direct message from each element about how they can guide you in the month ahead. And you can work with any of your other favorite oracle decks for divination.

You can dance to anchor your intentions. This will energize them in the physical body. You can add pictures and art to your journal to connect to the messages visually as well as verbally. To add even more energy to your new moon seeding times, you can create a simple ceremony around your intentions.

Remember to keep a record of your progress and date each new moon journal entry. You might also find it helpful to write down notes about your awarenesses as you experience the new moon energy. Pay special attention to the kinds of things that rise to the surface of your consciousness during the new moon time. The day before the new moon, the day of the new moon, and the day after the new moon all provide you with a window of opportunity to do seeding work with your co-creations. At these times, you will find the energy most beneficial for bringing desires into physical form.

Between the new moon and the full moon, a two-week period of growth and outer-focused energy occurs, called the waxing phase of the moon. It is important to work with anything you want to increase during this time. Once the full moon occurs, the moon begins its waning cycle, and the energy begins to turn inward for reflection. Anything that needs to be released to allow your co-creations to occur is best completed during this time.

Intentions of the Solar and Lunar Astrological Gates

(Dates for each sign are approximate)

♈ *Aries – Fire: Spring Equinox, March 21- April 19.*
Apply individual will. Be yourself. Energize desires. Get more exercise and move more. Start projects. Fire up desires. Take action. Connect to your inner warrior. Make time for sports and play activities. Move things forward. Accomplish tasks. Birth something new.

♉ *Taurus – Earth: April 20- May 20*
Beautify your home, garden, and wardrobe. Enjoy earthly and bodily pleasures. Develop patience. Create grounded goals and strategies. Develop wealth-growing skills. Manage finances. Care for your body. Develop dependability. Relax and enjoy life.

♊ *Gemini – Air: May 21 - June 20*
Connect to creative ideas. Develop networking skills or network. Make public relations efforts. Accomplish writing and speaking projects. Develop communication. Work with your imagination. Create change. Explore something new. Take on artistic and creative projects. Gather information.

Cancer – Water: Summer Solstice, June 21- July 22
Nurture self, family, friends, and projects. Apply love where needed. Create comfort. Birth what has been gestating. Care-take home and domestic life. Connect with family and friends. Care for your emotional needs. Heal your inner child. Support the young. Play near the water.

Leo – Fire: July 23 - August 22
Activate your radiance. Fill yourself with self-love. Turn up your inner fire. Increase self-confidence. Fire up your zest for life. Celebrate accomplishments. Develop the courage to follow your heart. Fine tune your presentational style. Enliven your stage presence.

Virgo – Earth: August 23 - September 22
Organize your life. Handle details. Perform ceremonies. Connect to the sacred. Increase productivity. Activate your sacred work. Be of service. Develop exercise and health programs. Tie up loose ends. Be useful. Connect to the patterns, rhythms and cycles of nature.

Libra – Air: Autumnal Equinox, September 23 - October 22
Balance relationships. Honor others' points of view. Integrate opposites. Consider options and choice. Mediate and create peace. Develop cooperative social skills. Host an event. Partner personally or professionally. Be a good companion. Think and write.

Scorpio – Water: October 23 - November 21
Feel all your feelings. Develop emotional maturity. Deepen psychic power, intuition, and sixth sense. Source life force. Transform and regenerate. Learn to manage intensity. Release what no longer serves you. Connect to sexual energy. Bring shadow to consciousness.

Sagittarius – Fire: November 22 - December 21
Expand whatever you focus on. Shine light on truth within. Evolve consciousness. Travel or plan to explore new territory. Study philosophy. Freely search for the meaning of life. Apply energy to what is ready to grow and develop. Learn and teach.

North

New Moon

Waxing Crescent

Balsamic

Sagittarius

Capricorn

♑

Aquarius

♒

MIDNIGHT

Winter Solstice

Scorpio

♏

Samhain

Imbolc

Pisces

♓

First Quarter

West

Last Quarter

Libra

♎

6:00 PM

Autumnal Equinox

Spring Equinox

6:00 AM

Aries

♈

East

Virgo

Lughnasad

Beltane

Taurus

♉

Disseminating

Leo

♌

Summer Solstice

NOON

Cancer

♋

Gemini

♊

Gibbous

Full Moon

South

The Wheel of Sacred Timings

Capricorn – Earth: Winter Solstice, December 22 - January 19
Responsibly create structure and form. Design and administrate systems. Develop procedures. Handle business and financial affairs effectively. Apply discipline to the physical world. Teach systems and structures. Create goals. Provide support for family and children.

Aquarius – Air: January 20 - February 18
Innovate. Experiment. Liberate. Bring in radically progressive original ideas. Gain insight and cosmic perspective. Launch new ideas. Explore unconventional and unique systems. Create your own way of doing things. Take risks. Revolutionize.

Pisces – Water: February 19 - March 20
Develop a loving, caring, compassionate heart. Serve humanity. Intuit your night dreams and day-dreams. Create art and poetry. Take time for renewal. Contemplate. Pray. Meditate. Visualize. Introspectively connect to your inner and spiritual world.

Full Lunar Tempo

Begin moving to the full tempo only if you feel comfortable with the first rhythm of the Wheel of the Year and the half tempo of the moon cycle, or if you feel you want to add another layer to how you are already working with the elemental energies. Remember to work with your desires and intentions one or two at a time. Just like learning dance steps, working with too many at one time can be overwhelming. When you are ready to add the next layer to your moon work, you can begin to dance to the rhythm of the full moon as well.

Full Moons

At a full moon, the energy of the moon's growing period reaches its cyclical peak. The intense energy shows you how well you worked with your intentions up to this point. This natural rhythm helps you conduct an evaluation of your progress so you can determine if you need to do anything additional to bring your desires into form. The waning cycle begun by the full moon reminds you to do your inner work needed to bring your desires to fruition.

The moon is full in the sign directly opposite the sun on the Astrology Wheel.

Aries opposite Libra

Taurus opposite Scorpio

Gemini opposite Sagittarius

Cancer opposite Capricorn

Leo opposite Aquarius

Virgo opposite Pisces

At the full moon, the sun and moon are opposite one another and directly influencing each other. So you can choose to either just work with the moon energy or you can work with the energies of both the sun and the moon astrological signs. At an Aries full moon, the sun would be in Libra. The Libra sun would highlight your relationships, so at the full moon you might explore how your individuation affects your relationships. You might possibly discover how your child ego affects your relationships, perhaps by being too demanding of others or by wanting its way all the time. The two archetypal energies of both sun and moon work hand-in-hand here. You can work with them together or simply focus on the moon's energy.

If you add the layer of the full moon rhythm to your co-creational dance you will want to record your discoveries in your journal, date those entries, add any additional notes, and possibly conduct a ceremony.

In order to assist you in your layered learning process, a lesson plan follows. You can use it to determine where you need to proceed next in your co-creational dance training.

Lesson Plan

As with learning any type of dance, your co-creational dance training requires that you increase your skill one step at a time and layer by layer. This lesson plan allows you to design your training based on your interest and pace. Feel free to leave out any steps or layers your inner guidance does not align with. Work with the number of steps you feel comfortable with and practice them one or two at a time until they feel smooth or graceful, then when you feel ready add the next step or full layer.

Layer One: Connecting to the Elements and Spirit

Step One: Learn to identify the voice or feeling of Earth, Water, Air, Fire, and Spirit externally.

Step Two: Learn to recognize each elemental voice internally.

Step Three: Learn to identify Spirit's voice in you - your essence self.

Step Four: Build an elemental altar and practice gratitude for each of the forces of nature.

Layer Two: Application of Elements

Step One: Learn to recognize when you need clearing with an element or when you need to apply the elemental powers co-creationally.

Step Two: Learn to use at least one clearing tool for each element (see Clearing Tools this chapter).

Step Three: Activate each element's primary power and practice using them co-creationally (see elemental chapters).

Step Four: Practice applying the elemental clearing and co-creational tools in daily life.

Layer Three: Holding a Unified Field

Step One: Activate each element's level two power and activate the unified field (see elemental chapters).

Step Two: Practice aligning the elements in a unified field with Spirit and notice which elements need additional attention in your co-creations.

Step Three: Practice giving gratitude and requesting assistance from the elements when you need a deeper understanding of your life.

Step Four: Practice calling in sacred space and using the elements in a simple personal ceremony.

Layer Four: Natural Rhythms Sacred Timings for Co-Creation

Step One: Practice working with the Wheel of the Year.

Step Two: Practice working with the Moon Rhythm.

Step Three: Practice working with the 12 Astrological Gates of Awareness through the year and/or month.

Step Four: Increase your coordination through practice and attention and give thanks.

Co-Creational Coordination

As you learn to smoothly align your unified field and instinctively move to the natural rhythms, you develop your co-creational coordination. Your unified field comes into alignment as your essence self flows through the physical, emotional, mental, and action realms. People who have developed their professions or crafts to their fullest know a time comes when what they do becomes natural and grace-filled, when their skills become strong and the energy flows through them, when they are in harmony with their craft. This is an aligned, unified field.

Learning to align your unified field, develop your skills, and move in life in a coordinated flow takes time. Until that happens, the important thing is for you to keep going. Nature frequently takes a long time to bring something into full, beautiful bloom. Be patient, keep taking steps to move forward, keep practicing and exploring new rhythms. As with anything that you are learning to coordinate, practice is key and sometimes finding a good teacher, support person, mentor, or supportive peer learning group makes a huge difference in your learning curve.

Co-creational dance requires that you learn to dance in alignment with your unified field to the rhythm of celestial music. The timing of the celestial music supports your co-creations as you discover how to move to its melody. When you know how to move to its timings, you will experience even more energetic natural support for your co-creations. For example, if you focus your co-creational dance during the time when a new or full moon lines up with a Wheel of the Year point, your desire may move into form much more quickly than it might have had you worked with your intentions at some other time. Such times also are especially potent for ceremony. If you want to fine-tune your ceremonial timing on a particular day, you can plan to do it around sun or moon rise, or sun or moon set, thus aligning with the natural rhythm of the day to add energy to your ceremony. Doing so, you add another layer of alignment to energize your co-creational intentions. The more you honor the energies and their alignment in the natural world, the more you deepen your capacity to co-create and bring forth both your personal and collective desires.

Although your goal revolves around conscious alignment with the energies, sometimes you line up with the energies without any conscious awareness of doing so. You simply live your life and enter a window of "magic." When this happens, you can see you do not have to believe in the timings and rhythms for them to work with and for you. They simply occur. You can tap into their energy because it exists, not necessarily because you are trying to do so, and you can choose to align with these natural forces anytime you want their support for your life.

To prove this, let me tell you a true story of someone very dear to my heart. He knew nothing of the natural rhythms, but lined up with them beautifully. Imagine a man who has been a master fisherman for years. He knows how to line up his physical skills to catch fish. He knows how to energetically flow with both his skill and the environment. He knows how to focus his mind, and he can take the right actions to catch fish. One day he and a friend chartered a boat and they went fishing out on the ocean, during the full moon window on Beltane. They started casting their rods just as the sun was rising. They spent that day and the next day catching fish, after fish, after fish. Each day they caught so many fish that they exceeded the limit and needed to release the surplus. They had a wonderful time catching their bountiful harvest. These two men had no idea that the full moon on Beltane supported their fishing in that window of magic. Without realizing it, they aligned the energy of their unified field with the celestial timing. When I heard the story and saw the amazing photos of all the fish they had caught, it was easy for me to understand what had happened. They had aligned with the elements and moved with the natural rhythms and fishing magic happened.

Now that you know how to align your energies in a unified field and to move to the natural rhythms of the universe, you don't have to wait for magic to happen. You can help to make it happen by aligning with the elements and natural rhythms, and then watch as your co-creations appear in form. You can dance gracefully with Spirit and the elements to the timing of the Wheel of the Year, the moon, and the astrological wheel as your intentions easily fall in place around you. Such grace comes from the high level of coordination achieved when consciously working with and moving to the natural rhythms. When you practice doing so, you too can achieve the rhythmic grace of a seasoned and well-trained dancer and dance to the rhythms of nature.

Co-Creation Worksheet

Feel free to copy this work sheet for your own personal use.

Date: _____

My desire from Spirit: _____

What I currently know about the form it will take: _____
_____

My intention: _____

How I feel when it is complete: _____
_____

The actions I need to take are: _____
_____
_____
_____
_____
_____

Additional guidance: _____
_____
_____
_____
_____
_____
_____
_____
_____

Anchored in ceremony on (date): _____

New moon seeded on: _____

Dates I have re-energized this co-creation and additional guidance I have received:

1. _____
_____
_____
_____

2. _____
_____
_____
_____

3. _____
_____
_____
_____

4. _____
_____
_____
_____

Date of the co-creation completion: _____

Feelings: _____
_____
_____
_____
_____

Dear Reader,
as you further your work with a unified field and the
natural rhythms of co-creation...

May your
life be harmonized to the sacred pulse of the universe
and bring greater essence expression to your dance.

May your
creations be nourished with deep love from an open-hearted space
as you celebrate your body and the beauty of the physical realm.

May your
passion for your life fuel action toward your desires as you gently
blow upliftment beneath your wings to soar to your dreams.

May your
abilities to work with a unified field expand
so that all of your co-creations
are filled with balanced grace.

With deep heartfelt blessings for the dance of your life.

NATURAL RHYTHMS™
INSTITUTE

Workshops, Trainings, and Degree Programs

Lisa Michaels - *Founding Director*
Cherie Lyon - *Assistant to the Director*
www.naturalrhythms.org
info@naturalrhythms.org

The Natural Rhythms Institute offers workshops, trainings, and degree programs. Our study areas include: Natural Rhythms, Practical Priest/ess, Synergistic Alchemy, and Specialization Programs. A variety of courses are offered within each of these programs and certificates of completion are awarded at the end of each level. Certified facilitators around the country offer some of these programs, while others are only offered periodically at the Natural Rhythms Institute in Atlanta, GA.

Natural Rhythms™

The Natural Rhythms™ Program functions as the foundation of the Natural Rhythms Institute. It is designed to develop your capacity to work with the elemental forces, their expression in the astrological gates of awareness, and their natural rhythm cycles. As you activate each element's power and its wholeness integration, your ability to design and align your life with the natural forces of co-creation dramatically increases.

Practical Priest/ess™

The Practical Priest/ess™ Program facilitates deeper access to the inner well of wisdom and awareness. It also increases the participants' direct connection to the Divine. Activating the Priestess or Priest within assists participants in bridging the world of Spirit and the earthly realm of matter. It is open to participants of all religious, cultural, and spiritual backgrounds. The Practical Priest/ess provides useful and workable spiritual tools and practices for everyday life. Based on the work of Nicole Christine and Lisa Michaels.

Synergistic Alchemy™

The Synergistic Alchemy™ Program intentionally activates the human body as the alchemical vessel of transformation. Each stage of Alchemy works with the elemental forces in the body and consciousness, interacting with one another to activate the transformational process. When the energy of alchemy is not blocked and instead activated, opened, and allowed to work, it clears and transmutes the personality so a deeper connection to Spirit can come through and express.

Specialization Programs

The Specialization Programs current subject categories include: Dance, Shamanic Practices, Ancestors, Natural Healing Tools, Creativity, Astrology, Facilitator Trainings, Natural Rhythms Life Coaching.

Please check our website www.naturalrhythms.org
for current program offerings.

FACILITATORS

Natural Rhythms™ Charter Facilitators

Georgia

Leslie Clayton
404-252-7550
lclayton@naturalrhythms.org
www.naturalrhythms.org

Judy Keating
404-790-4508
jkeating@naturalrhythms.org
www.naturalrhythms.org

Susan F. Kersey
770-653-9857
skersey@naturalrhythms.org
www.naturalrhythms.org

Cherie Lyon
404-735-9631
cherielyon@naturalrhythms.org
www.naturalrhythms.org

Lisa Michaels
770-717-5190
lisamichaels@naturalrhythms.org
www.naturalrhythms.org

Bonnie Salamon
706-219-1020
bsalamon@naturalrhythms.org
www.naturalrhythms.org

North Carolina **Donna Marlene Richardsen**
828-582-0200
drichardsen@naturalrhythms.org
www.naturalrhythms.org

Ohio **Tammy Huber-Wilkins**
513-231-3030
thuberwilkins@naturalrhythms.org
www.naturalrhythms.org

Lynette McCormack
513-759-2091
lmccormack@naturalrhythms.org
www.naturalrhythms.org

Paula York
859-653-7298
pyork@naturalrhythms.org
www.naturalrhythms.org

Please check our website www.naturalrhythms.org for our current facilitator list and offerings in your area.

Disclaimer: Each Natural Rhythms™ Facilitator functions as an independent business owner and uses the Institute's training materials and methods in all associated Natural Rhythms™ programs they facilitate. Each Natural Rhythms™ Facilitator is solely responsible for their own business and facilitation environments. The Natural Rhythms™ Institute assumes no liability for their independent facilitation or business practices.

For those interested in learning about a Priest/ess Process please see the facilitator list below. There may be additional facilitators in your area. Many Priest/ess facilitators also travel from their local areas to present the process.

Priest/ess Process **Nicole Christine,** *Priest/ess Process™ Creatrix*
www.magdalenemysteries.com
nicole@magdalenemysteries.com
Available for private phone or in person sessions.
See website for more information.

Priestess Process Facilitators

The following Natural Rhythms Charter Facilitators also facilitate a variation of the Priest/ess Process, see their connect information above.

Georgia **Judy Keating**
Susan Kersey
Cherie Lyon
Lisa Michaels

Ohio **Paula York**
Tammy Huber-Wilkens

North Carolina **Anyaa McAndrew** *MA, NCC, LPC*
828-788-0773
anyaa@verizon.net
www.goddessontheloose.com

Georgia **Shari Starrfire**
404-625-4668
sharelight@mindspring.com
www.sharistarrfire.com

ACKNOWLEDGMENTS

Thank you, to this book's amazing designer and illustrator, and my precious life partner, Prescott Hill. From this work's inception your talent for powerful visual images has repeatedly given life to my ideas. Our creative collaboration and your loving support provides the air under my wings for my work, play, and life to soar.

Thank you to my mother, Lorine and my father, Bill for loving me into this world, so that my life and this book could have expression.

Thank you to Cindy, Cheri, Lee, Kevin, Kim, Jeff, Brennan, Lauren, Patrick, Elizabeth Ann, Cheryl, Charles, and Elizabeth P. for all the ways you've loved, supported, and taught me in life.

Each of us learns through our life experiences, so thank you to all those who have crossed my path as formal or informal teachers.

Thank you to Nicole, Bonnie, and Nina for all your long hours of work editing, proofing, and assisting me in the process of writing. Each one of you brought something necessary in the development of the book.

Thank you to each of you whom I have had the pleasure of teaching or facilitating in a dance class, workshop, or process. You each added to the material presented here by allowing me to share, to keep growing with the work, and by contributing your energy and insights.

Thank you to Cherie Lyon who repeatedly coached the birthing process of both the book and the Institute. I give abundant gratitude to all the charter Natural Rhythms Facilitators, Bonnie, Cherie, Susan, Judy, Donna, Lynette, Paula, Leslie, and Tammy. Each of you has gone the extra mile to support and share this work.

Thank you to Great Spirit, the Elemental Forces, and the Archetypes for your constant and unwavering inner guidance and teachings.

And to Dance, you have made it joyous to be in physical form expressing the Divine within.

NOTES

Introduction: Natural Rhythms

1. Nicole Christine Priest/ess Process 1997. www.magdalenemysteries.com

2. Gregg Braden, *Awakening to Zero Point* (Bellevue, WA: Radio Bookstore Press, 1997)78.

Chapter One: Dance of Creation

1. Genia Pauli Haddon, *Body Metaphors: Releasing God-Feminine in Us All* (New York: Crossroad Pub Co, 1988). Later re-titled *Uniting Sex, Self & Spirit* (Scotland, CT: Plus Publications, 1993)18-23. In the early 90's this book profoundly changed my view of the expression of yin/yang energies.

2. Ibid., 18-23.

3. Daniel Giamario and Carolyn Brent n.k.a. Cayelin K. Castell, *The Shamanic Astrology Handbook* (Tucson, AZ: JCAU Publications 2004). Shamanic Astrology forms my foundation for understanding the astrological signs from an archetypal perspective. The astrological information in this book draws on the wisdom of Shamanic Astrology and integrates a more general use of astrology as well. www.shamanicastrology.com

Chapter Three: Earth

1. Juan Nuñez del Prado Peruvian Andean Initiation Journey, 1998.

2. Wheel of the Year References:

Cait Johnson and Maura D. Shaw, *Celebrating the Great Mother* (Rochester, VT: Destiny Books, 1995).

Edain McCoy, *The Sabbats: A New Approach to the Old Ways* (St. Paul, MN: Llewellyn, 1994).

Starhawk, Diane Baker, and Anne Hill, *Circle Round: Raising Children in*

Goddess Tradition (New York: Bantam Books, 1998).

3. Chakra References:

Anodea Judith, Ph.D., *Wheels of Life: A User's Guide to the Chakra System* (St. Paul, MN: Llewellyn, 2001).

Anodea Judith & Selene Vega, *The Sevenfold Journey: Reclaiming Mind, Body, & Spirit Through the Chakras* (Freedom, CA: The Crossing Press, 1997).

Caroline Myss, Ph.D., *Anatomy of the Spirit: The Seven Stages of Power and Healing* (New York: Harmony Books, 1996).

4. Patti Conklin Workshop 1998. www.patticonklin.com

5. Nicole Christine Priest/ess Process 1997.

Chapter Four: Water

1. Gregg Braden, *Walking Between the Worlds: The Science of Compassion.* (Bellevue, WA: Radio Bookstore Press, 1997)99-146.

2. James Redfield and Carol Adrienne, T*he Celestine Prophecy An Experiential Guide* (New York: Warner Books, Inc., 1995)88-89.

3. Eckhart Tolle, *A New Earth: Awakening to Your Life's Purpose* (New York: Penguin Group, 2005).

4. James Redfield and Carol Adrienne, *The Celestine Prophecy an Experiential Guide* (New York: Warner Books, Inc., 1995)88-89.

5. Ibid.,89.

6. Juan Nuñez del Prado Peruvian Andean Initiation Journey, 1998.

7. Gregg Braden's *Awakening to Zero Point Workshop* Mid 90s. www.greggbraden.com

8. Lucia Capacchione, Ph.D. *Recovery of Your Inner Child* (New York: Simon & Schuster / Fireside, 1991).

9. Jean Ann Burger's Class Mid 80s.

10. Juan Nuñez del Prado Peruvian Andean Initiation Journey, 1998.

Chapter Five: Air

1. Robert Tennyson Stevens' Workshop 1995. http://www.masterysystems.com

2. Jean Ann Burger's Class Mid 80s.

3. Daniel Giamario and Carolyn Brent n.k.a. Cayelin K. Castell, *The Shamanic Astrology Handbook* (Tucson, AZ: JCAU Publications 2004). Shamanic Astrology forms my foundation for understanding the astrological signs from an archetypal perspective. The astrological

information in this book draws on the wisdom of Shamanic Astrology and integrates a more general use of astrology as well.

4. Gregg Braden, *The Isaiah Effect: Decoding the Lost Science of Prayer and Prophecy* (New York: Three Rivers Press, 2000).

Chapter Six: Fire

1. Gregg Braden, *Walking Between the Worlds: The Science of Compassion.* (Bellevue, WA: Radio Bookstore Press, 1997)136.

2. Cait Johnson and Maura D. Shaw, *Celebrating the Great Mother* (Rochester, VT: Destiny Books, 1995)191.

Chapter Seven: Spirit

1. Gregg Braden, *The Isaiah Effect: Decoding the Lost Science of Prayer and Prophecy* (New York: Three Rivers Press, 2000)100-101.

2. Genia Pauli Haddon, *Uniting Sex, Self & Spirit* (Scotland, CT: Plus Publications, 1993)18-23.

3. Nicole Christine Priest/ess Process 1997.

4. Ibid.

Chapter Eight: Elemental Tools

1. Juan Nuñez del Prado Peruvian Andean Initiation Journey, 1998.

2. Nicole Christine Priest/ess Process 1997.

Additional Resources

These books and sites represent only a few of the vast additional selection of resources available to assist your elemental and natural rhythm journey.

Earth

Durek, Judith. *Circle of Stones: Woman's Journey to Herself.* Novato, CA: New World Library, 2004

McNeill, Mackey Miriam. *The Intersection of Joy and Money.* Ft. Wright, KY: Prosperity Publishing, 2002.

Starck, Marcia. *Women's Medicine Ways: Cross-Cultural Rites of Passage.* Freedom, CA: The Crossing Press, 1993

Water

Bays, Brandon. *The Journey: A Practical Guide to Healing Your Life and*

Setting Yourself Free. New York: Fireside, 1999.

Bradshaw, John. *Healing the Shame That Binds You*. Deerfield Beach, FL: Health Communications, Inc. 1988.

Britten, Rhonda. *Fearless Living: Live Without Excuses and Love Without Regret*. New York: Berkley Publishing Group, 2001.

Hendricks Ph.Ds, Gay and Kathlyn. *The Conscious Heart: Seven Soul-Choices That Create Your Relationship Destiny*. New York: Bantam Books, 1997.

Ruskin, John. *Emotional Clearing: An East/West Guide to Releasing Negative Feelings and Awakening Unconditional Happiness*. R. Wyler & Co; Rev Exp. edition, 2006.

Tipping, Colin C. *Radical Forgiveness: Making Room for the Miracle*. Marietta, GA: Global 13 Publications, Inc. 2002.

Vitale, Joe. *Zero Limits: The Secret Hawaiian System for Wealth, Health, Peace, and More*. Hoboken, NJ: John Wiley & Sons, Inc. 2007.

Air

Douglas-Klotz, Neil. *Prayers of the Cosmos: Meditations on the Aramaic Words of Jesus*. New York: HarperSanFrancisco, 1990.

Kenyon, Tom. www.tomkenyon.com

Melchizedek, Drunvalo. *The Ancient Secret of the Flower of Life Volume 1 & 2*. Flagstaff, AZ: Light Technology Publishing, 1990 & 2000.

Castell, Cayelin K. www.celestialtimings.com

Fire

Jenkins, Elizabeth B. *Initiation: A Woman's Spiritual Adventure in the Heart of the Andes*. New York: The Berkley Publishing Group, 1997.

Noble, Vicki. *Shakti Woman: Feeling Our Fire Healing Our World ~ The New Female Shamanism*. San Francisco, CA: HarperSanFrancisco, 1991.

Stevens, Jose Ph.D. & Lena S. *Secrets of Shamanism: Tapping the Spirit Power Within You*. New York: Avon Books, 1988.

Spirit

Braden, Gregg. *The God Code: The Secret of Our Past, the Promise of Our Future*. Carlsbad, CA: Hay House Inc, 2004.

Cameron, Julia. *The Artist's Way: A Spiritual Path to Higher Creativity*. New York: G.P. Putnam's Sons, 1992.

Christine, Nicole. *Under Her Wings: The Making of a Magdalene*. Bloomington, ID: AuthorHouse, 2005.

Hendricks, Gay. *Conscious Living: Finding Joy in the Real World*. New York: HarperSanFrancisco, 2002.

Kryder, Rowena Pattee. *Gaia Matrix Oracle*. Mount Shasta, CA: Golden Point Productions, 1990.

Monk-Kidd, Sue. *Dance of the Dissident Daughter*. San Francisco, CA: HarperSanFrancisco, 2002.

Rose, Sharon. *The Path of the Priestess: A Guidebook for Awakening the Divine Feminine*. Rochester, VT: Inner Traditions, 2002.

Alchemy
Hauck, Dennis William. *The Emerald Tablet: Alchemy for Personal Transformation*. New York: Penguin Group, 1999.

Henry, William. www.williamhenry.net

Price, John Randolph. *The Alchemist Handbook*. Carlsbad, CA: Hay House, 2000.

Dance/Rhythm
Andes, Karen. *A Woman's Book of Power: Using Dance to Cultivate Energy and Health in Mind, Body, and Spirit*. New York: The Berkley Publishing Group, 1998.

Redmond, Layne. *When the Drummers Were Women: A Spiritual History of Rhythm*. New York: Three Rivers Press, 1997.

Roth, Gabrielle. *Sweat Your Prayers: Movement as Spiritual Practice*. New York: Penguin Putnam Inc., 1997.

Stewart, Iris J. *Sacred Woman, Sacred Dance: Awakening Spirituality Through Movement and Ritual*. Rochester, VT: Inner Traditions International, 2000.

Accelerated Learning
International Alliance for Learning. www.ialearn.org

Heidenhain, Gail. www.delphin-international.com

ABOUT THE AUTHOR

Lisa Michaels, author, dancer, facilitator, and founder of the Natural Rhythms™ Institute, assists others in accessing their ability to learn from nature and to discover more about their essence expression. For the past twenty years she has shared her expertise through her products, workshops, and facilitator trainings. Lisa's most current products include her new book *Natural Rhythms™, Priestess Within, The Elemental Forces of Creation Oracle* and *Audio Book.* Her work has helped thousands of people find the key to moving their lives forward, thus enlivening their ability to co-create and unlocking their natural growth potential. Lisa makes in her home and garden near the sacred site of Stone Mountain with her creative live partner Prescott.

ABOUT THE ILLUSTRATOR

Despite a steady diet of animated cartoons, Three Stooges and comic books as a child, Prescott Hill somehow grew to appreciate and embrace the finer magical aspects of visual communication early on. Growing up, he experimented with all forms of eye-candy including theater, set design, photography, animation, and filmmaking. Graduating in 1979 from The New England School of Art and Design in Boston, Prescott has spent the past twenty nine years pursuing a career as a master graphic designer and illustrator, discovering his spiritual path through the process of his work. He makes his home in Atlanta by the side of his dear life partner, Lisa Michaels and is in royal servitude to their two cats, Will and Grace. His portfolio is online at www.prescotthill.com

PRODUCTS BY LISA MICHAELS

Priestess Within: Your Direct Divine Connection

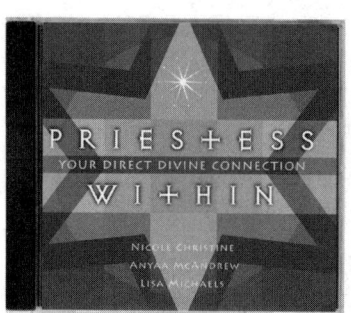

The Priestess archetype teaches you to become the empty vessel, the chalice, the hollow bone. From this inner state of receptivity, you bring forth the subtle vibrations of divinity. As a priestess in these times, you connect to the Earth as your Living Temple and come to know that by simply living your life you are performing a sacred act. The Priestess Within by Nicole Christine, Anyaa McAndrew and Lisa Michaels is a tremendous tool to assist you in opening and deepening your direct connection to the divine.

Compact Disc   **ISBN 0-9715994-3-2**

The Elemental Forces of Creation Audio Book

The elemental forces of creation are powerful guides in understanding the magic that happens when you bring forth your essence desires, then prepare the fertile soil of your life, mix it with your clear flowing emotional water, the alignment of your belief system and the power of your actions. When you work with all the elements in such an aligned way, you literally vibrate your desire into being. It is important in the process of learning to create that you develop the skill to work with the elements individually as well as together.

A Four Compact Disc Set   **ISBN 0-9715994-1-6**

The Elemental Forces of Creation Oracle

This unique set of 90 full color Elemental cards, created by Lisa Michaels and illustrator Prescott Hill, comes with a 44-page manual. The oracle guides you into a living relationship with the elemental wisdom of Earth, Water, Air, Fire and Spirit. Each element is a powerful teacher of consciousness. They work with you to increase your inner knowing, develop deeper self-awareness, and actively expand your life expression.

A 90-card Oracle Deck   ISBN 0-9715994-2-4

Natural Rhythms™ Sacred Timings Poster

A full color, 12" x 18" laminated presentation poster of the "Sacred Timings" illustration found in this book on page 242. Perfect for facilitation or personal use. *Designed and Illustrated by Prescott Hill.*

12" X 18" Full Color, Laminated   **ISBN 0-9715994-5-9**

*These products are available at select bookstores,
on line at www.naturalrhythms.org
and from the fine folks at www.sacredspaces.org.*

INDEX